Battleground Europe

Somme

LA BOISSELLE

Ovillers/Contalmaison

P

sl

R

T

S

W

L

With the continued expansion of the Battleground series a **Battleground Series Club** has been formed to benefit the reader. The purpose of the Club is to keep members informed of new titles and to offer many other reader-benefits. Membership is free and by registering an interest you can help us predict print runs and thus assist us in maintaining the quality and prices at their present levels.

Please call the office 01226 734555, or send your name and address along with a request for more information to:

Battleground Series Club Pen & Sword Books Ltd,
47 Church Street, Barnsley, South Yorkshire S70 2AS

Battleground Europe
SOMME

LA BOISSELLE
Ovillers/Contalmaison

Michael Stedman

Series editor
Nigel Cave

LEO COOPER

By the same author:

Salford PALS
Manchester PALS
Somme - Thiepval
Great Battles of the Great War

First published in 1997
Reprinted 2003

LEO COOPER
an imprint of
Pen Sword Books Limited
47 Church Street, Barnsley, South Yorkshire S70 2AS

Copyright © Michael Stedman 1997, 2003

ISBN 0 85052 540 3

A CIP catalogue of this book is available
from the British Library

Printed by CPI UK

For up-to-date information on other titles produced under the Leo Cooper imprint,
please telephone or write to:
Pen & Sword Books Ltd, FREEPOST, 47 Church Street
Barnsley, South Yorkshire S70 2AS
Telephone 01226 734555

CONTENTS

INTRODUCTION BY SERIES EDITOR

This is the fourth book in the Battleground Europe series to cover a part of the old July 1st 1916 front line. In it Michael Stedman examines the actions of units and individuals as they battled around the small Somme villages of La Boisselle, Ovillers and Contalmaison on that first day and in the subsequent wresting battle that followed to secure them. Such narratives, perhaps not in such detail, have existed before, but now they are put firmly in the context of the country over which they were fought and the lasting memorials that have remained. These latter range from the dramatic excavation in the ground caused by a mine and which is now known as Lochnagar Crater to the beautifully secluded cemetery at Becourt to the poignant stone that commemorates the place near which Captain Francis Dodgson fell on 10th July 1916. Any visitor will have a much clearer idea of what happened in this small part of the Somme front once they have read this book and walked the routes that it recommends.

La Boisselle therefore stands scrutiny as both a guide and a narrative within which the topography of the ground and the events which unfolded here are examined in detail. Within the text more than twenty maps, much unique illustrative material as well as a number of evocative contemporary descriptions have been placed to enhance your insight and understanding of these remarkable places.

What those visitors will not learn from this book is why the battle was fought; the series has set itself limited objectives for a variety of reasons. There already exist excellent books about the origins of the battle and the conduct of grand strategy. I would particularly recommend General Anthony Farrar-Hockley's masterly but short *The Somme*. Martin Middlebrook's *The First Day on the Somme* remains the outstanding book of its type, using a large number of veterans' reminiscences to provide an outstandingly readable book which attempts to apply a more human interpretation to a bald military narrative. Historians may differ about their interpretations and explanations, but these books provide a good starting point to a more detailed understanding of the battle.

Although eighty years on, the controversy about the conduct of operations in the Great War is as alive and well as it has ever been – perhaps best shown by the considerable media interest in the eightieth anniversary commemorations on the Somme and in the number of radio and television programmes about the battles and the decision makers that were also shown in that year. The interest amongst the public is clearly illustrated by the demand for these books.

The 1916 Battle of the Somme was fought for a variety of reasons and was the result of compromises as to location and as to the size of the effort. It was the biggest battle ever fought by a British Army, which in turn was the biggest army that the nation had ever put in the field. This was a nation inexperienced in major military continental entanglements, and however much critics may complain about the callousness of talking about a 'learning curve', the fact of the matter is that this was what the Somme became. A citizen army, based to a large degree on an urban population, full of naive enthusiasm became an experienced, battle hardened force. Soldiers, in many cases for the first time, learned the horrors – and techniques – of modern warfare. The technical arms, and in particular the artillery, learnt more about the potential and limitations of their own weapons. Generals learnt about the limitations of detailed planning and the problems of assaulting massively prepared defensive positions and wrestled, with means to overcome these. Politicians learnt the cost of war and set in motion ever greater efforts to provide the industrial base to support the military machine; they also tried to find alternatives to fighting the major enemy on the major front, without success.

The plan for July 1st was ambitious, the objectives were highly optimistic. Decisions and suppositions made by Rawlinson, the field commander, by Haig, his commander in chief and by various other players have rightly come in for detailed examination, sometimes highly critical. What has been noticeable by its absence is similarly detailed examination and criticism of the actions of the French and German commanders. The casualty figures for the German army during the Battle of the Somme are hotly disputed; on some figures they lost approximately the same, on others about two thirds of the allied casualties. Whatever the truth, the fact remains that the German army suffered huge casualties during this battle. Was this because they, too, were an army led by so called 'donkeys'?

These books do not set out to answer any of these questions, but I hope that the reader will follow up his interest in the battlefield with a wider reading of the issues involved. The soldiers of the Great War deserve better than to be considered as the mere playthings of 'indifferent and callous commanders'; and these latter deserve a far more objective judgement of their performance.

NIGEL CAVE
Ely Place, London

INTRODUCTION

The twin villages of La Boisselle and Ovillers are almost always associated, in the minds of their many visitors, with the awful hours which followed on from the blowing of the Lochnagar and Y Sap mines at 7.28 am on the 1st July 1916. This is not surprising. Those events were indeed cataclysmic, seminal moments in the military history of Britain's New Armies. But the history of La Boisselle, Ovillers and Contalmaison during the summer months of 1916 hides many a forgotten battle and moments of great heroism and fortitude which often lie undisturbed along history's convoluted wayside paths. One of my aims within this guide is to redress that imbalance.

The enduring mental anguish and memories of the fighting on the Somme battlefields moved many men to write with an authority and power which the passage of time has not in any way diminished. Anticipating the distant future whilst writing in 1929, Charles Douie, whose terrible sojourn began here at La Boisselle before moving further north to Thiepval, wrote that, "For many years to come stray travellers will revisit the ground where once they fought and endured, where many of their friends lie for ever. But the time must come when the travellers are seen no more, and only the forest of graves above the Ancre will remain to tell the tale of that island race whose sons once were lords of these woods and fields." Today the different interpretations which people, who often have no experience of conflict, place on such words can mean that Douie's understanding of the war can seem out of place in a Europe changed far beyond that distant soldier's imaginings. However,

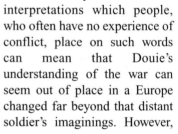

Operating a Vickers machine gun near Ovillers during the opening days of the Battle of the Somme, July 1916. They are wearing gas hoods and both men have spoons stuffed into the tops of their leggings.

it would be an ill-advised person who sought to avoid the many and varied lessons of history. Those who claim that "the path to the future is not through the past" often come to regret such words. By the same token there is of course no golden age to which we can or should return, but to shun consideration of the bleakest or best episodes in man's experience will only breed falsity and weaken the foundations of the future.

In this context La Boisselle is one of life's finest classrooms and it is possible to see many visiting groups and individuals sampling the extraordinary history here. A common failing of many such visits is a tendency to attempt too much. First stop Serre, then Newfoundland Park and onto Thiepval for lunch, followed by La Boisselle, Pozieres and the Butte de Warlencourt before returning to the hotel in Arras, exhausted and perhaps little the wiser! And tomorrow will be Ypres. Yet such places are powerful, evocative and emotionally exhausting, especially for the young upon whom they can make a great impression. To skimp them is like 'doing' Westminster Abbey in five minutes. To trivialise by rushing will simply undermine what could be learned. You cannot marvel at, learn from and treasure the new understanding of something when you are exhausted, and the Somme battlefield is no exception. Much better to halve your itinerary and manage the time you can have here sensibly. Get to know this magnificent location of La Boisselle in depth. Let careful observation and thoughtful questioning reveal the many layers of fact, insight and interpretation to yourself, your school party or your family and friends.

Of course, La Boisselle sees thousands of passing motorists every day. Amongst them many British vehicles pass speedily by the site of the Glory Hole, eschewing interest in the site of Y Sap mine, casting barely a glance across the confines of Mash Valley as they leave to cross the wide skylines formed by the Tara – Usna hills towards Albert or the Pozieres ridge in the direction of Bapaume. Every school student now knows that La Boisselle and Ovillers possess a terrible yet magnificent history of great tragedy on the 1st July 1916, but many enthusiasts now pass by, en route for Pozieres, High Wood or some other place of supposedly greater interest to be reached from the D929. It is as if La Boisselle has become the essential first port of call on any initial visit to the Somme, drawn by the one magnet which attracts thousands of visitors into this village each year, Lochnagar Crater, La Grande Mine. Yet all too often those first visits are brief, simply an opportunity to be staggered by the enormity of the crater. This is a great pity because La Boisselle and the nearby villages of Ovillers, Becourt and Contalmaison encompass a great wealth of history, encapsulating the pathos, bravery, sacrifice and endurance which have become bywords for the soldiers'experience during the Battle of the Somme. It is therefore my intention, through the pages of this guide, to reveal that the fighting here had a far greater significance than is often imagined. The battle for La Boisselle waged by the Butterfly Division, the 19th, is often forgotten yet in truth is a climacteric event which determined much that happened during the coming weeks and months of the Somme campaign. The battle for Ovillers raged for a fortnight, drawing many British and German divisions into its vortex of horror and attrition. Without the capture of Contalmaison the extraordinary events of the great dawn attack on 14th July, made on the German second line positions around Bazentin and Longueval, could never have taken place. This area will therefore repay a carefully prepared visit many times over with its wealth of interest and insight.

MICHAEL STEDMAN
Leigh, Worcester

Australians machine gunners, in the foreground, pass a working party going up to the front line. The ruined village of Contalmaison can be seen in the background.

Acknowledgements

Within the narrative record of events here at La Boisselle I have made considerable use of those many words, often penned in haste amidst terrible danger more than eighty years ago. To all of those soldiers who wrote at that time and those who penned their memoirs during the post war era I am grateful and can only stand in awe. However, it would have been impossible to complete this guide without the help of many of my contemporaries. In particular I should like to thank Nigel Cave who has undertaken a thorough review of this work and for whose sensible help, guidance and suggestions I am very grateful; Bob Bonner and Ron Young, Dr Dick Edmonds, Charles and Reggie Fair, Michael Kean-Price, Jerry Gee and Derek Butler and other staff of the Commonwealth War Graves Commission at Maidenhead, Peter Hart, Paul Reed, John and Nancy Rogers, Geoff Thomas, Ralph Whitehead, Colonel Lowles of the Worcesters' Regimental HQ together with Mike Nicholson, Katie Doar and Phil Nash of Waterstones' Booksellers whose excellent specialised maps department, at 17 St Ann's Square, Manchester, supplied my maps and through whom the requisite present day IGN maps of France can be obtained. The staff at the Public Records Office in Kew have also provided me with much help, assistance and considered judgement. Many members of the Western Front Association have helped in greatly enhancing my knowledge of the La Boisselle area. To all of these people I should like to extend my sincere thanks whilst making clear that any errors which remain within the text are solely of my own making.

Sensible equipment and advice for visitors

I have heard it said that war can be defined as 'a catastrophic and heartrending event which takes place at the meeting of more than one map'! La Boisselle and the nearby villages of Ovillers and Contalmaison challenge every visitor and Frenchman in this respect since the villages and their nearby farmland are handily located near to the conjunction of no less than four IGN series maps. I hope therefore that this pocket guide will, if nothing else, make life easier for those of you ever tempted to unfold such numerous sheets in the face of driving wind and rain on the Pozieres ridge overlooking La Boisselle and Ovillers.

One of the greatest pleasures, and the most salutary and moving of experiences, is to 'walk the course' of an event in the extraordinary history of the Great War, reconstructing in our minds the encounters of the men who were there and sharing the chance insights and discoveries with friends. For me, like so many other people, the first course was that fatal and tragic route taken by the Newfoundlanders. Later came the Salford Pals, below Thiepval. But whoever you are following, or whatever you are trying to explain and understand, certain items are always likely to enhance your pleasure. It is worth noting that here in the La Boisselle area there is relatively little shade and some of the walks I have described may take a whole morning or afternoon. Therefore, sun cream and plenty of drinks are essential. Stout shoes or walking boots at any time of the year are vital. Wellington boots and thick socks in winter or soon after rain are needed, along with appropriate outer clothing. A compass is an essential, together with a trench map and comparable present day map. For those enthusiasts spending longer in the field and who want to record your visit carefully some further items are advisable. A camera; a pen and notebook to record where you took your photographs, and perhaps to note your visit in the cemetery registers. A drink, a sandwich, a decent penknife with a corkscrew, a first aid kit and a shoulder bag for everything.

Here in La Boisselle, as at Thiepval, a metal detector is, let us be frank, an embarrassment. To be seen digging within sight of what should be a place of tranquillity and reflection is almost to desecrate the memory of those whose names are recorded so starkly on the Memorial to the Missing which dominates the skyline to the north. The spectacle of lone Britons sweeping their electronic plates across empty fields fills me with sadness. This is a place where a more rewarding and significant history reveals itself, without recourse to indignity.

No significant preparation is required to cope with medical requirements. It is however very sensible to ensure that you carry an E111 form which gives reciprocal rights to medical and hospital treatment in France, as well as all other EC countries. The necessary documents can be obtained free from any main post office. As in the UK where you are in a working agricultural area and may be scratched or cut by rusty metals, ensure that your tetanus vaccination is up to date. Comprehensive personal and vehicle insurance is advisable, at the very least Green Card insurance (often available free from your vehicle insurers) is certainly sensible when motoring abroad. In this context it is worth noting that there have been an increasing number of thefts from British tourists' vehicles in the area of the Somme, even when parked near to the many cemeteries and features around La Boisselle. To help arrange and plan your stay I have identified a list of campsites, hotels and B&B accommodation within easy distance of La Boisselle in Chapter 1, which deals with the designated area today. However, a fuller guide to the many excellent hotels, restaurants, auberges and overnight accommodations available in the Picardie area can be obtained from the *Comite Regional du Tourisme de Picardie*, 3 Rue Vincent Auriol - 80000 Amiens - Tel: 00 33 322 91 10 15.

How to use this book

This guide can be used in preparation for your visit, in front of the fire at home on a cold winter evening. In that case it is perhaps best read from start to finish. I think you will have a sound feel for La Boisselle at the end of one or two evenings' reading and might be ready to book your cross channel ferry or tunnel for those days in March and April when the weather begins to clear, the fields are ploughed and crop growth has not yet hidden the detail and topography of the ground. But the guide is also designed as a pocket reference, a quick supplement to your knowledge when you are 'walking the course' and need an explanation or clarification.

By far the best way to see the La Boisselle, Ovillers and Contalmaison area is on foot or bicycle. At the end of the text you can find a number of suggested routes making use of the paths and tracks which are accessible to these means of transport. The two chapters dealing with 1916's historic events within the designated area are obviously in chronological order. Although there was conflict here during the spring of 1918 this guide is not intended to cover that conflict since it will be the subject of a further volume in this series. The chapter dealing with cemeteries is constructed in alphabetical order and follows after a description of the memorials which are also identified and described within the same section.

I suggest that a tour by car or coach is the best way to get your bearings and to give an overview of the whole area. Again I have suggested a tour to highlight the main features of the area, along roads which are easily accessible. The roads covered by this suggestion are usually quite satisfactory for coaches and involve no dangerous turns through 360^{0}! This tour is also to be found at the end of the book and is strongly recommended to those of you not already conversant with the area. It is worth noting that some of the tracks and smaller roads to be found on the IGN maps of the area are not suitable for coaches. Cars without four wheel drive will find difficulty in getting along some minor tracks, for example that leading from Fricourt to La Boisselle past Lochnagar crater. Be prepared to walk is the best advice that I can give, but do take care to lock all valuables, especially cameras and other inviting items, out of sight in the boot of your vehicle.

On the subject of maps

Here in the vicinity of La Boisselle the most useful maps are the IGN Blue Series to a scale of 1:25,000 entitled *Albert West* (2408 *ouest*) and *Bray-sur-Somme* (2408 *est*). For those of you interested in the detail covered by the northern part of this guide Bapaume East and Bapaume West (2407 *est et ouest*) will also prove a sensible purchase. Taken together these four maps cover the entirety of the British sector of the 1916 Battle of the Somme. The IGN Green Series 1:100,000 will also help you find and navigate the area by car.

Below I have identified the maps which appear within this guide. For most navigational and walking purposes these will be sufficient for your enjoyment of this area. However, for a really intimate knowledge of each location the 1:10,000 and 1:5,000 trench maps are indispensable to the serious student or expert.

You should note that the trench maps, which are available from the Imperial War Museum Department of Printed Books (tel: 0171 416 5348) or the cartographer of the Western Front Association (members only), follow a specific sequence and should be referred to by the numbers usually found in their top right hand corner. The most useful map covering the La Boisselle area is the 1:10,000 scale sheet: Sheet 57D. S.E. 4, entitled Ovillers, (which covers the Authuille, Aveluy and Albert areas, as well as Ovillers, La Boisselle, Contalmaison and Pozieres.) Variously dated versions are available from both sources. In the text I have sometimes referred to locations which are noted on such trench maps, but not on present day maps. In such cases I have where necessary given the relevant trench map reference to help you identify the exact position. For example, 'Y Sap' at La Boisselle is located on sheet 57D. S.E.4 at map reference X.13.d.5,5. Since almost everything described within this guide is located on sheet 57D. S.E.4., I will normally omit that prefix to any map reference.

However, one feature which the young or first time visitor might wish for is an easily accessible reconstruction which gives an insight into the conditions which prevailed around La Boisselle and Ovillers at the height of the conflict. One such source of insight and empathy is to be found at Newfoundland Park, two miles north-west of Thiepval on the Auchonvillers road out of Hamel, the D73. This is an area of preserved battlefield, purchased by the government of Newfoundland after the Great War. Unfortunately the lie of the land at Newfoundland Park cannot easily translate into an understanding of the terrible mud and devastation which surrounded the commune of La Boisselle in the mid summer of 1916. However, further detailed insight can be obtained at the two quality museums which are within reasonable distance. The first, at Albert below the celebrated Basilica, is only ten minutes away by car. The second, the 'Historial' at Peronne, is well worth the longer

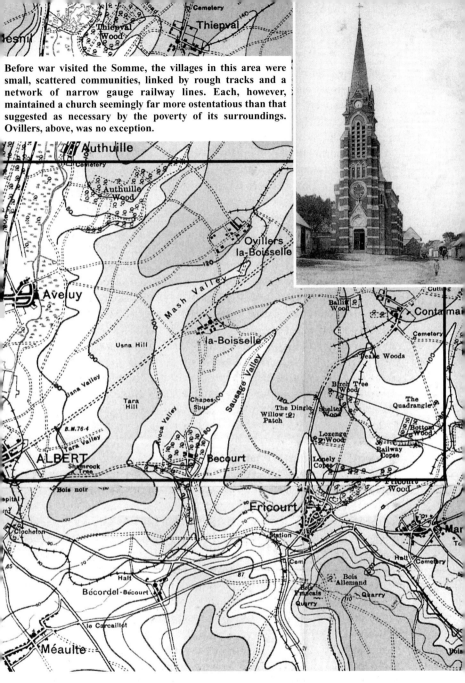

Before war visited the Somme, the villages in this area were small, scattered communities, linked by rough tracks and a network of narrow gauge railway lines. Each, however, maintained a church seemingly far more ostentatious than that suggested as necessary by the poverty of its surroundings. Ovillers, above, was no exception.

Map 1. The La Boisselle / Ovillers / Contalmaison battlefield area, showing the pre-war settlements and geography of the area. This is taken from the 1;40,000 sheets which accompanied the Official History volume detailing the fighting leading to the first day of the Battle of the Somme.

journey, but you should remember to set aside a good forty minutes travelling time, each way. Take the D938 running south-east from Albert to Peronne, a route which will enable you to follow the southern arm of the British front lines as they existed before the the Somme battle.

One extraordinary fact about the Somme and Ancre battlefield is that after the utter devastation of the Great War many of the tracks and other human geographical features were reconstructed in the 1920s with an uncanny similarity to their pre-war locations. Most of the pre-1914 and trench maps of the Ovillers – La Boisselle area still stand true today, although some minor variations have occurred south of La Boisselle towards the Avoca Valley and Tara Hill. Initially the processes of reconstruction were almost insurmountably difficult. In order to help, many of the villages were adopted by some of Britain's towns and cities. Here, in the case of Ovillers – La Boisselle, some responsibility for the village's restoration was taken on by the city of Gloucester. On 23rd October 1922 the Mayor of Gloucester formally placed in the possession of the villages two windmill water pumps and reservoirs as the basis of the re-established water supply. That civic gesture was reciprocated in October of 1925 when, during a visit by representatives from the village of Ovillers, a wreath was laid at the Gloucester War Memorial. In 1996 I could find no remnants of this historic link.

However, in the early 1920s, as more villagers returned to rebuild their homes and lives with the reparations monies wrung from Weimar Germany, every effort was made to find the exact location of their pre-war houses. Sometimes, when a villager did not return that plot was left vacant, in many cases still so today! But, we should remember that Ovillers, La Boisselle and Contalmaison are working villages, communities whose roots are based in centuries of toil on the land which is also our place of interest. This is not 'open access' land on the National Trust model. It is all too easy to let our two interests clash. During the autumn months, in particular, be aware of the numerous shooting parties. The farmers will not welcome the sight of your tramping the fields with little regard to crops and seeds. Please ask before you enter. Please keep to the paths and to the edges of each field. Remember, a trench map in your hand does not entitle you to unlimited access across the area depicted, no matter how interesting it may appear as we wander

Chapter One

OUR DESIGNATED AREA TODAY

The straight road running from Albert to Bapaume, the D929, neatly bisects what was the British sector of the first Battle of the Somme. The village of La Boisselle therefore lies in the very centre of this axis, along which it was planned to execute the 'Big Push'. However, much of the fighting north of that road in the summer, autumn and early winter of 1916 was influenced by the course of the River Ancre which has created a steeper and more substantial sequence of valleys and slopes. Walking to the highest points on the Ovillers spur will give you fine views across this more rugged scene bordering the Ancre valley, west towards Aveluy and north towards Thiepval.

Behind the battlefield lay the town of Albert, familiar to almost every British soldier who served during the first 'Battle of the Somme'. Today Albert describes itself as being only the '*3eme Ville de la Somme*', but quite properly '*la Cite d'Ancre*'. The Town Hall square in Albert often hosts a market and there are three small supermarkets nearby which can all provide a sound array of food and refreshments. However, the area due east of Albert past Becourt, south of La Boisselle and on towards Contalmaison is more undulating, gentle countryside, filled with seemingly endless fields dotted with tiny distant woods. This is an area within which it is easy to lose any sense of direction and my hope is that this guidebook will provide an authoritative and interesting companion in your search for understanding and clarity. Outside Albert the village of La Boisselle is just three kilometres distant along the D929 road leading towards Bapaume. The village of Ovillers is one kilometre to the north of La Boisselle. There is a busy roadside cafe, 'The Poppy', as you approach La Boisselle from the direction of Albert. However, this cafe does not provide rooms.

The first thing you might therefore need to arrange is accommodation and tomorrow morning's breakfast. Since it lacks accommodation La Boisselle is not the place to stay when visiting the area! I have therefore identified below some of the nearby hotels and a number of 'English' B&B style houses where you can base yourself during a visit. However, for those of you with a tent or caravan and a more adventurous disposition, the 'Bellevue' campsite in Authuille is a fine and central point on the Somme battlefield which can be reached from Ovillers – La Boisselle in less than ten minutes by car. Take the road to Aveluy adjacent to La Boisselle's communal cemetery and from

Aveluy the D151 to Authuille. The campsite is quiet and often frequented by people who share an interest in the Great War. The owner, Monsieur Desailly, and his family are always welcoming. Recently the Bellevue campsite has been expanded to include a simple restaurant, reached thirty yards to the right of the main campsite entrance, where the food is both substantial and economical. Here you are within two minute's walk of the Authuille Military Cemetery and not far from the *Auberge de la Vallee d'Ancre* on the banks of the River Ancre. For many years this bar and restaurant has served decent food and drinks for as long as you cared to stay! The Auberge has been taken into new ownership recently (1995) by Denis Bourgoyne who has already established a fine reputation for the quality of his food amongst the local community.

However, it can be bitterly cold camping in February! Therefore, for those of you who are travelling in style or during these colder and wetter months of the year, a roof over your heads may be welcome. The list identified below may be of some help, but it should not be inferred that the order is one of descending merit! To call for reservations from the UK dial 00 33, followed by the 9 digit number. In all these hotels, with one exception in Picquigny, you will find at least one person on the hotel's staff who can speak English.

Hotels:
The Royal Picardie ***, Route d'Amiens, 80300 Albert. Tel 322 75 37 00.
The Hotel de la Basilique **, 3 - 5 Rue Gambetta, 80300 Albert.
    Tel 322 75 04 71.
The Relais Fleuri **, 56 Avenue Faidherbe, 80300 Albert. Tel 322 75 08 11.
The Grande Hotel de la Paix *, 43 Rue Victor Hugo, 80300 Albert.
Tel 322 75 01 64.
Les Etangs du Levant *, Rue du 1er Septembre, 80340 Bray sur Somme.
Tel 322 76 70 00.
Auberge de Picquigny **, 112 Rue du 60 R.I., 80310 Picquigny.
Tel 322 51 20 53.
Hotel Le Prieure. 17 Route National, 80860 Rancourt. Tel 322 85 04 43.

B&B style accommodation:
Courcelette. A distinctive family farmhouse, self catering or meals provided. 'Sommecourt' is situated right at the heart of the 1916 Somme Battlefields. Plenty of facilities including guided tours and a small but fascinating museum. This fine location almost has the Ovillers / La Boisselle area on its doorstep.

Paul Reed and Kieron Murphy. Sommecourt, 39 Grande Rue, 80300 Courcelette. Tel: 322 74 01 35.

Auchonvillers / Beaumont Hamel. Very comfortable and well appointed accommodation for up to ten people. Attractive grounds and very interesting walks nearby. Evening meals and continental breakfast. Perhaps ten to fifteen minutes from La Boisselle driving past Newfoundland Park and Thiepval.

Mike and Julie Renshaw. Les Galets. Route de Beaumont, Auchonvillers. Tel: 322 76 28 79.

Auchonvillers. Five good rooms with en suite facilities and an extremely interesting history, the centrepiece of which is the cellar still carved with the names of many soldiers who passed through in 1916. Bed, breakfast and evening meals by arrangement as well as a Tea Room for non residents. Again, access to La Boisselle best undertaken by car.

Avril Williams. 10 Rue Delattre, 80560 Auchonvillers.

Tel: 322 76 23 66.

THE AREA OF LA BOISSELLE

Once you are established it is time to see the surrounding locality and I suggest that, soon after you arrive, you would enjoy following the general tour explained in Chapter 6. However, in this first chapter I have attempted to give some definition to the boundaries of this guidebook and give a brief commentary to illustrate the importance of the area's history. Whilst you drive it will become clear that the area around Ovillers and La Boisselle is gently undulating chalk-land, devoid of the harsher features created by streams or rivers. The valleys which meander here seem innocent, but their confines provided no cover for the inexperienced New Army Tommies of 1916. Further to the north, beyond the scope of this guide, three substantial woods in the vicinity of Thiepval provided more effective cover as well as a measure of camouflage prior to the assaults which took place there on 1st July 1916. Here at La Boisselle far less woodland was available, although that at the foot of Chapes Spur surrounding the chateau at Becourt was both influential and is today still littered with trenches, interest and insight.

The area dealt with by this guide is that which came under the command of III Corps for the purposes of the attacks which took place here on 1st July 1916. III Corps was commanded by Lieutenant-General Sir W.P. Pulteney. There were three divisions under his command; the 8th commanded by Major-General H. Hudson, the 34th commanded by Major-General E.C. Ingouville-Williams who was later killed in action on 22nd July and the 19th Division, commanded by Major-General G.T.M. Bridges. Beginning in Albert the Corps' chain of command stretched north towards Aveluy before turning north east to pass through the south-eastern fringe of Authuille Wood. The left boundary of III Corps then continued north-east cutting across the road running from Thiepval towards Pozieres and skirting 200 metres south of Mouquet Farm. The main German Second Position ran along this higher ground through Mouquet Farm, north towards Grandcourt and south-east towards Pozieres. On the left of III Corps the 8th Division was assigned the difficult task of capturing Ovillers, their first objective, then advancing to take the main German Second Position south of Mouquet Farm and then taking Pozieres as their third and final objective. These two divisions would therefore move forward at zero in order to ascend the rising ground leading up towards their allotted segment of the Thiepval – Pozieres – Ginchy ridge. The most obvious military difficulty which they faced was the consequence of geography, the two spurs of higher land which pointed from the ridge down into the 8th and 34th Division's sectors. In order to understand the military history of the battle here it is essential to have a clear mental picture of the area's distinctive topography. These spurs were the Ovillers Spur and the Chapes Spur upon which stood La Boisselle. Between the two spurs ran Mash Valley. Of the two spurs Ovillers is by far the most significant. From Ovillers there is ample observation well past the town Albert and further westwards. To the north of the Ovillers Spur, past Blighty Valley, stood the Leipzig Salient on its own dominant spur. To the south of Chapes Spur, past Sausage Valley, stood the high ground running down from Contalmaison towards Fricourt. Consequently any advance along these valleys was bound to be assailed by enfilade fire from the higher ground either side of any progress. It was a daunting prospect.

This however is not the place to recount the events which unfolded in front of Ovillers and La Boisselle that bright morning on 1st July 1916. Suffice to say that, in view of the disastrous casualties incurred by all units serving with III Corps, the plan was incapable of being fulfilled and this guide will therefore use the upper reaches of Blighty (or Nab) Valley as its northern perimeter, thence running south to the road junction (X.8.b,6,7) 200 metres north-east of Ovillers[1]. From that location a road and track then travel south-east in the direction of Contalmaison, crossing the Albert - Bapaume road half way between La Boisselle and Pozieres. The village of Contalmaison therefore provides the easterly limits of this guide. From Contalmaison the D147 Fricourt road runs along the south-eastern boundary of the guide. However,

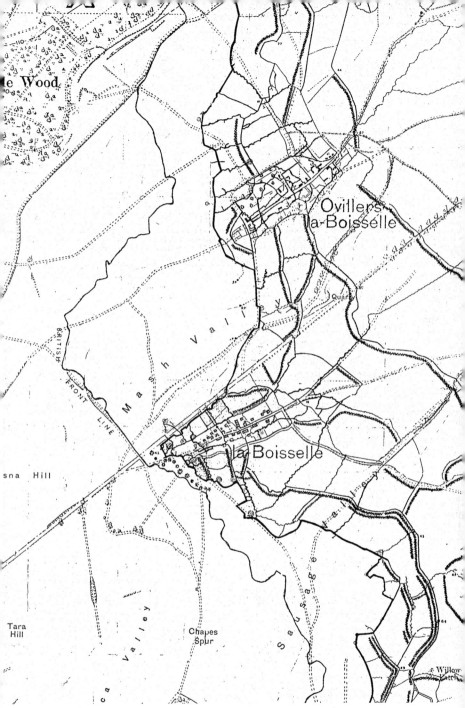

Map 2. The German trenches at La Boisselle and Ovillers, drawn from the British 1:10,000 trench map of the area corrected to 7/2/1916.

before that road turns southwards in the direction of Fricourt our area of interest continues westwards past the 'Willow Patch' (marked as the Bois de Becordel on IGN maps) and thence to Becourt and its surrounding woodland.

The right boundary of III Corps on 1st July 1916 was therefore a line running from Becourt to Contalmaison past Peake Woods. The division which was entrusted with this sector was the 34th Division, which included the Tyneside Scottish and Tyneside Irish Brigades. The casualties experienced by this division became a byword for the terrible experience suffered by the British Army that morning. The first objectives of the 34th Division's men lay some 2000 metres to the east of La Boisselle. Their second objectives were the German defences on the west of Contalmaison, their third objective a line running from the east of Contalmaison towards the east of Pozieres. In an act of stunning fortitude and bravery some soldiers belonging to the 24th and 27th Northumberland Fusiliers, part of the Tyneside Irish Brigade, actually penetrated as far as Contalmaison that morning.

The boundary between the two divisions of III Corps ran just north of Usna Redoubt (surmounting the Mont d'Ancre on IGN maps) along the track which then crosses the La Boisselle - Aveluy road (X.13.a. 2,3). On the other side of that La Boisselle - Aveluy road the track continues as a properly metalled road running past the British Military Cemetery into Ovillers. However, that road past Ovillers cemetery lay within the 8th Division's area and the boundary between the 8th and 34th Divisions can be visualised running from the cross roads (in X.13.a) due east towards the chalk quarry between Ovillers and La Boisselle (X.14.b.3,9).

The twin villages of Ovillers and La Boisselle. Separating the two villages is Mash Valley. View looking north eastwards from behind the British Front Line.

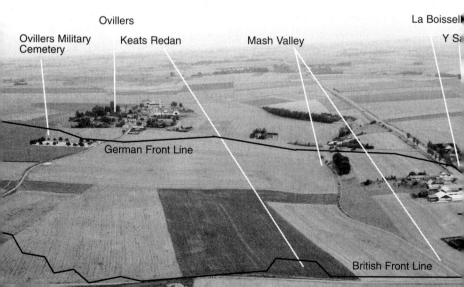

Ovillers

La Boissell▮

Ovillers Military
Cemetery

Keats Redan

Mash Valley

Y S▮

German Front Line

British Front Line

La Boisselle

Site of Y Sap

Keats Redan

The village of La Boisselle, seen across Mash Valley from the site of Keats Redan (X.13.c.8,7) on the British front line adjacent to the La Boisselle - Aveluy road

The significance of the failure of the attacks on the Ovillers – La Boisselle area lies in the geography of the German positions to the rear of those two heavily fortified positions. Ovillers and La Boisselle lay almost in the centre of the British sector of the Somme Battlefield and the Official History describes the 1st of July's events as the opening day of the 'Battle of Albert'. Perhaps that would have been better described as the First Battle for the Pozieres Ridge. As we have noted, at the end of the initial phase of fighting, that is zero plus two hours and forty minutes on 1st July, it was anticipated that British troops would have overrun Ovillers – La Boisselle and be in possession of the eastern perimeter of Pozieres. Had the attacks towards Grandcourt, Thiepval and Mouquet Farm gone according to plan in X Corps' area to the north of Ovillers then X Corps and III Corps would, between themselves, have opened up the higher ground along the whole Thiepval – Pozieres Ridge giving artillery observation and parity for the subsequent phase two assaults on High Wood and Delville Wood along the southern part of that ridge towards Ginchy. Had those two woods been captured quickly that would have then enabled artillery control over the incomplete German Third positions around Flers and Le Sars in front of Bapaume. Such an early British success would almost certainly have forced a reappraisal of German tactics, any German counter attacks being forced to come from relatively disadvantaged positions below British positions of strength. Such a situation would have reduced the need for those costly and incremental advances by which the British Army then crept slowly across the Thiepval – Pozieres – Ginchy Ridge during the autumn and early winter period of late 1916.

1. Mouquet Farm and Pozieres will be dealt with in further guides as part of this series.

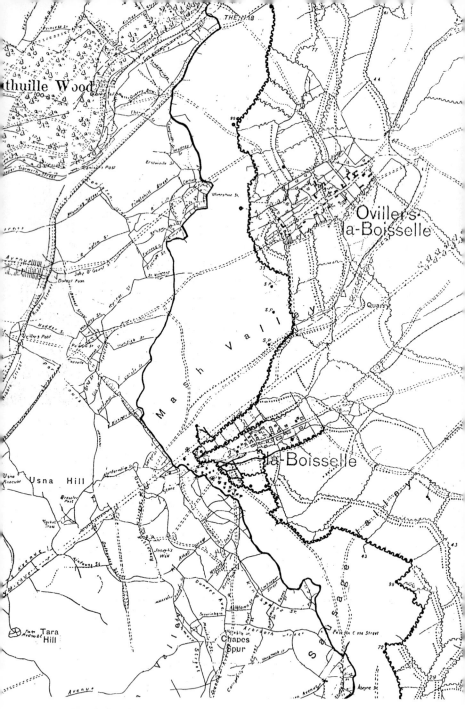

Map 3. Detail from a trench map corrected to 27/4/1916 showing La Boisselle and Ovillers.

Chapter Two

THE BRITISH PERSPECTIVE TO JULY 1916

Arrival!

With the approach of winter at the end of 1915 the British troops in this sector began to understand the impact which the area's geography would have upon them during the coming months. Facing Ovillers the drainage position was helped by the slope of the land, but in front of La Boisselle the trenches were situated in a hollow running from Mash Valley down into Avoca Valley and on towards Becourt. There, as autumn deepened into winter, the water slowly and irreversibly dissolved the chalk into which the trenches had been cut, creating a slimy ooze which adhered to any and everything with which it came into contact. Shallow breastworks had necessarily taken the place of many waterlogged trenches. These positions were amongst the most evil and filthy within which any unit could be expected to serve on the Western Front. A young officer like Charles Douie, on a first reconnaissance visit for his platoon, Number 1 of A Company of the 1st Dorsets, 14 Brigade of 32nd Division, would find the place to be a daunting experience.

Charles Douie

'We passed down our front-line trench towards the ruins of the cemetery through which our line ran. East of the cemetery was the heaped white chalk of several mine craters. Above them lay the shattered tree stumps and litter of brick which had once been the village of La Boisselle. We progressed slowly down the remains of a trench and came to the craters, and the saps which ran between them. Here there was no trench, only sand-bags, one layer thick, and about two feet above the top of the all-prevailing mud. The correct posture to adopt in such circumstances is difficult to determine; we at any rate were not correct in our judgement, as we attracted the unwelcome attentions of a sniper, whose well-aimed shots experienced no difficulty in passing through the sand-bags. We crawled away and came in time to a trench behind the cemetery, known as Gowrie Street. Liquid slime washed over and above our knees; tree trunks riven into strange shapes lay over and alongside the trench. The wintry day threw a greyness over all. The shattered crosses of the cemetery lay at every angle about the torn graves, while one cross, still erect by some miracle, overlooked the craters and the ruins of La Boisselle. The trenches were alive with men, but no sign of life appeared over the surface of the ground. Even the grass was withered by the fumes of high explosive. Death, indeed, was emperor here.'[1]

By extraordinary chance, the cross which Douie saw survived all the shellfire of June and early July to be discovered, still upright and complete, when the British finally wrested control of the village!

Having survived that first experience and achieved the sanctuary of relief the officers and men had then to retreat down one of two notorious communication trenches which served the La Boisselle positions. The first of these was St. Andrew's Avenue which led across Usna Hill just yards to the north of the Albert – Bapaume road. The second was Berkshire Avenue which led eastwards from the relative safety of Albert, across the exposed southern part of Tara Hill into the filthy mud swamped confines of Avoca Valley. On making that first journey out Clifford Platt, an officer serving with the third of Salford's Pals Battalions which also formed part of 14 Brigade, wrote that:

'....this morning's journey down a trench called Berkshire Avenue, which leads from the trenches to A—[lbert], was the worst part of the whole show. It is just a mile long, and we took four solid hours to get to the end: nearly the whole way along there is thick sticky clay up to one's knees and on this occasion I had on a Burberry stretching nearly down to my ankles!'

A Raid

No matter how demanding the physical conditions were it was always necessary to maintain some semblance of the Offensive Spirit. Such an ideal was deemed necessary for good morale. Whether an optimistic outlook was always achieved is difficult to say, but raids did provide vital information about the enemy's dispositions and the state of his readiness and defences. One such raid, by the 32nd Division, took place in the late winter weather of early 1916.

On the morning of Sunday 6th March 1916 the area of La Boisselle was still shrouded in snow. At dawn, as the men stood to arms in sub zero temperatures, their breath formed clouds of vapour, crystals of condensed moisture growing on their tunics and weapons. Later, between the hours of 9.00 and 11 am, rain fell steadily, making underfoot conditions even more treacherous. It was just thirteen hours before the raid on Y Sap, whose objective was to test the strength of the defences and to capture prisoners for identification purposes, would

German front line trench in the hollow of Mash Valley between Ovillers and La Boisselle. See photograph on page 96.

This card, postmarked '25th February 1915' and sent by a soldier of 26th Reserve Division, shows the *Verpflegungsstation der I Komp. Res. Rgt. N. 120. 1914. La Boisselle.*

begin for the 1st Dorsets. The enterprise would be led by Captain Algeo, with Lieutenant Mansel-Pleydell and 2nd Lieutenants Blakeway and Clarke.

In the evening the practice ground at Millencourt, laid out with tapes representing the German trenches at La Boisselle, was attacked again as it had been on many recent evenings. The charade was designed to reassure any watching German spies that nothing was afoot. The reality was that the Germans seemed well aware of impending events. For some days German artillery had registered the British lines opposite La Boisselle. By late evening a machine gun in Ovillers' dark ruins would occasionally traverse the British positions around Keats Redan and opportunistic whizz-bangs were exploding. Overhead, flares were being launched in the vicinity of La Boisselle with monotonous regularity. Charles Douie, witnessed the scene clearly in the crisp contrasts of a cloudless night sky.

'The broken posts and wire which marked the boundaries of No Man's Land and the white chalk of the mine craters were agleam in the moonlight, and it was so clear that I could discern the ruins and broken tree stumps of the village. Yet no shot was fired while a hundred men crawled through our wire into shell holes in front. Behind them the trenches were lined with men, for the 'Stand-to-Arms' had been passed down. The deathly silence did not augur well, and as the Colonel passed down the line I noticed grave anxiety on his face.'[2]

Three 'feeble' mines, set under the Glory Hole, were detonated by the RE at 12.25 am on the morning of 27th. It was five minutes too early and not all the raiders were in position. Again Charles Douie paints a vivid picture.

'The earth throbbed. Then again, but for one moment only, there was an unearthly stillness. This was succeeded by a weird sound like rustling leaves for a fraction of a second; then with the noise of a hurricane the shells passed, and the whole outline of the German positions was seared with the appalling lightning and thunder of our artillery. There were a thousand flashes, and a lurid light spread over the battlefield, the light seen only in that most dreadful spectacle, a night bombardment. The thunder of the guns was such that speech was impossible. But there was no time to observe the scene, as in an inferno of flashes and explosions the German counter-barrage broke on our lines.'

Nevertheless, the rush to get into the German position was underway. Lieutenant Mansel-Pleydell's party of 33 men rushed towards the tip of the La Boisselle trenches, next to the Route National, (at X.13.d.5,3), whilst the Y Sap party of 28 men, commanded by 2nd Lieutenant Blakeway, raced up the shallow slope below Y Sap. Ten men in support waited in No Man's Land (at X.13.d.3,5). A watching Sergeant Major felt uneasy that the Germans 'could not have retaliated quicker had they known of our plans, of which we came to the conclusion later they must have been fully aware.'[3] Every conceivable weapon had opened up on the ground across which the raiders were scurrying. But worse was to come. As the men leaped into Y Sap's trenches it soon became clear the place was empty. The trenches had been deepened and stretched with taut barbed wire. Many of the raiders became inextricably entangled. Within seconds a fearful German bombardment also began to fall on Y Sap itself – the raiders had been tricked into a cauldron of fire from which there was no easy escape. From either side a hail of grenades and 'oil cans' began to cascade upon the men struggling within the blackened confines of the deep trench. There was no point even in trying to press onto the German support trenches which were under British artillery fire. The order to retreat was sounded at 12.45 am. 2nd Lieutenant Blakeway, seeing one of his wounded men caught fast tried desperately to free him, only himself to become hooked and exposed.

Sergeant Major Shephard's diary recorded that as the men withdrew, from the confines of La Boisselle, they faced a,

'...terrible job to get disentangled from wire and all under a severe gruelling from trench mortars, whizz-bangs, etc. At 2.00 40 were still missing. At 2.30 am the [German] bombardment had lessened a good deal, and search patrols, stretcher bearers went out to find and bring in remainder. Four were found dead in

31

enemy trench, hopelessly tangled in wire, and impossible to move owing to heavy bombing. Wounded were got in, remainder of party got back to Usna at 3.00 am., and were issued with rum and tea. Their clothing was torn to shreds. They returned to Millencourt at 5.00 am. Great efforts were made until dawn to get in dead and find missing.'

Of the four officers involved 2nd Lieutenant Blakeway was killed during this raid. Captain William Algeo was killed soon after, at Thiepval on 17th May 1916, in the company of Lieutenant Henry Mansel-Pleydell. 2nd Lieutenant Clarke survived until 1918.

The Miners

Every contemporary account of life in the front lines at La Boisselle talks of the mining. The word became synonymous with La Boisselle. The great mine crater at Schwaben Hohe took its popular name from a British communication trench leading to the front line across part of Chapes Spur, Lochnagar Street (X.20.c.3,8). This was one of many colloquial titles which betrayed the earlier presence of Scotsmen here, men belonging to the 51st (Highland) Division which had taken over the trenches here from the French in 1915, and whose town and workplace names had given the miserable trenches the familiarity of home with names such as Abroath and Braemar Streets. Many feet below, ever since 1915, the soft chalk which provided the bedrock of the Somme battlefield had encouraged the miners in their constant subterranean war. Having arrived here for his first tour of duty in the sector Charles Douie wrote in awe inspired terms of the life of these miners.

'The one occupation which the infantry admitted to be more hazardous and less enviable than their own was that of the men whose daily lot was to descend the mine shafts in and around the cemetery of La Boisselle. I descended a shaft on one occasion, and although assured by the officer on duty that there was no safer place on the Western Front, I ascended again with remarkable speed, preferring the hazards of an open-air life in the mine-craters to the narrow galleries, driven above and below the German galleries, where men lay always listening to the tap of enemy picks, and waiting for the silence which was ever the prelude to the blowing of mine or counter-mine. The men of my regiment, being drawn from an agricultural community, had a particular dislike for mining fatigues. The miners themselves, for the most part following their traditional occupation, never appeared happy until they reached the mines.[4]'

The 'Glory Hole' today.

The Official History does give a brief description of the circumstances being faced by the miners here.

'This tunnelling in close proximity to the enemy was carried out in silence, with bayonets fitted with a special spliced handle; the men were barefooted; and the floor of the gallery was carpeted with sandbags. The operator inserted the point of the bayonet in a crack in the ìfaceî or alongside a flint, gave it a twist, and dislodged a piece of chalk, which he caught with his other hand and laid on the floor. If for any reason he had to use both hands on the bayonet, another man caught the stone as it fell. The dimensions of the tunnels were about four and a half feet by two and a half feet. An advance of 18 inches in 24 hours was considered satisfactory. The spoil was packed in sandbags and passed out along a line of men seated on the floor, and stacked against the side, ready for use later to "tamp" the charge.'

The trenches around the La Boisselle communal cemetery, at the junction between the Route National and the roads leading east and south towards Contalmaison and Becourt, were known to the British troops as the Ilot. The position was notorious for its insecurity and the proximity of the trenches. However, the main mining effort was being made by 179th Tunnelling Company of the Royal Engineers who, working from Becourt Wood, progressed steadily towards Schwaben Hohe during the early months of 1916. A similar effort was being made to undermine the 'Y Sap' position, raided by the Dorsets, whose imposing position overlooked Mash Valley on the northern side of the Albert – Bapaume road. In the days prior to the blowing of these two enormous mines the galleries were packed with 60,000 and 40,600 pounds of ammonal respectively[5]. Y Sap's mine was therefore of similar magnitude to that prepared by 252nd Tunnelling Company under Hawthorn Ridge, the detonation of which was so graphically filmed by

Geoffrey Malins from behind the sunken lane near Beaumont Hamel. Two other, smaller, mines were also prepared. These were each charged with 8,000 pounds of ammonal and were sited under the German positions opposite Inch Street, at the south-eastern end of the Glory Hole.

Final Preparations

For the ordinary British soldier, waiting for the Big Push was a difficult and emotional time. Many of these men had at least some intimation that the coming weeks would be a severe test of their resolve and military prowess. Although a great number were naive and confident, not all were so full of assured anticipation. Amongst the men of the 19th Division, who would be in support of the first day's attacks at La Boisselle, one such soldier was Private John Price. He had been placed into the 10th Worcesters even though his home was in Gloucester. Before the war he had been one of the 'Sammy's Angels', so called because all the employees of the Moreland's Excelsior Match works in Gloucester were notoriously short lived. This problem was especially true of those employees like John Price who worked in the mixing and dipping rooms where the overwhelming presence of phosphorous and sulphur almost inevitably led to the deadly industrial disease known as 'Phossy Jaw'. Fortunately John Price's health had been saved by the intervention of his girlfriend, Laurel, who had sworn she would never marry an 'angel' and had forced him to change to a new job before agreeing to their marriage!

On the 26th June John Price was just days from his appointment with destiny. It was only 48 hours since he had celebrated his birthday. Now, under canvas behind Albert, he wrote a letter which is full of sadness, revealing both his own grim mood and yet also his hopes in the event of his death. In some ways, in view of Private Price's despair and the references to his lice and war weariness, it seems surprising that this letter passed the company officer's censorious hand. However, the words are written in the west country dialect of a Gloucester working man and, most tellingly, their simplicity reveals the great love he feels for his family and home.

'26/6/16 .... I did not enjoy my birthday but I had a glass of beer but it was French beer not the good old English beer. My love you must buck up and cheer up and may God speed us back to the dear old home land again to free us all again my love. I ham not so Tickey that I was but I have got rid of a few of them, I suppose you know what I means, them little bits of dirt with legs on my love. I shall be glad when this war his all over. I ham got sick and tired of it all sometimes. It gets on my nerves my love. I dont want you to worry but keep a brave little heart and be merry and bright my love.'

On the reverse of the last page John Price wrote,

'Kiss to son From His Dearest Dad some were in France.
XXXXXXXXXXXXXXXXXXXXXXXXXXXXXXXXXXXX
Good Night.'

An extract from the letter written by Private John Price, 10th Bn. Worcester Regiment, on the 26th June, five days before the Battle for La Boisselle commenced.

The *Granatenhof* at La Boisselle. For a period of time prior to June 1916 a number of buildings remained as visible reminders of the village's pre-war agricultural purpose. But by the end of June there was little more than brick dust, low rubble and shattered leafless trees to mark the location of the village.

The German troops who suffered the bombardment of La Boisselle were men belonging to the 110th Reserve Regiment, 28th Reserve Division. The 110th Reserve Regiment held two battalions in the front line defences, the third battalion being held in reserve within the intermediate positions and the main Second Position. To the British observers and officers watching from near to their dugouts, a mere fifty yards north of the Albert Bapaume road on the Usna Hill, the German positions inside La Boisselle seemed, at first sight, to be receiving a terrible battering at the hands of the British artillery.

'From a distance the place looked like the mouth of a volcano, but the clouds of ascending smoke and dust flickering with the flashes of bursting shells prevented any actual view of the scene beneath. It looked at the time as if no Boche [sic] could possibly remain alive in such an inferno...'[6]

Contrary to popular conception the British bombardment had produced a substantial amount of damage in the forward German trench system. The German account of these final days of bombardment recalls that;

> 'Trenches and obstacles, weak dugouts and even the best observation posts were almost all destroyed. On the 29th June *Oberst Frhr*. Von Vietinghoff was buried in his battle head-quarters and suffered gas poisoning, however he remained in command which was transferred to the reserve battle headquarters in Contalmaison. Movement in the trenches was maintained only under the most extreme exertion, and their original course was hardly recognisable at times. The entrances to the few remaining deep dugouts were wrecked and could barely be kept open. It appeared the worst at the *Lehmgrubenhohe* [north west of Fricourt].'

Further north in the Ovillers sector the German troops belonged to the 180th (10th Wurttemberg) Regiment under the control of the 26th Reserve Division. The 180th had two battalions in the front line defences on the Ovillers spur and across the upper reaches of Nab Valley. Its third battalion was in the main Second Position north of Pozieres. The Official History calculated that the 8th Division's 9,600 men were therefore opposed by just 1,800 men of the 180th Regiment.

One British soldier who was desperately worried that the artillery preparations were insufficient was Lieutenant Colonel Edwin Sandys of the 2nd Middlesex. His battalion was due to attack the German trenches across the widest part of Mash Valley. Sandys knew that many German soldiers had survived the bombardment in their deep dug-outs[7] and made representations to his brigade and divisional staff. From an artillery observation post on Usna Hill Sandys spent many hours staring at the German wire, becoming increasingly morose and depressed. At night he was seen walking amongst his men's bivouacs, unable to sleep in his anxiety. However his fellow officers within the 2nd Middlesex did not share Sandys' concerns. They, like so many other New Army officers in this sector, felt that the attack would be an easy success.

The objectives set for the British assault to be undertaken by III Corps in this area were ambitious. The potential gains resulting from success were great. III Corps was commanded by Lieutenant-General Sir W.P.Pulteney and consisted of the 8th, 34th and 19th Divisions. The first objective north of Ovillers on the 8th Division's front was the western face of the Nordwerk and a line of trenches running south from there towards the north-eastern end of Ovillers village. From there the first objective line of the 34th Division ran towards Bailiff Wood and thence towards Peake Woods. Assuming success on the frontage to be

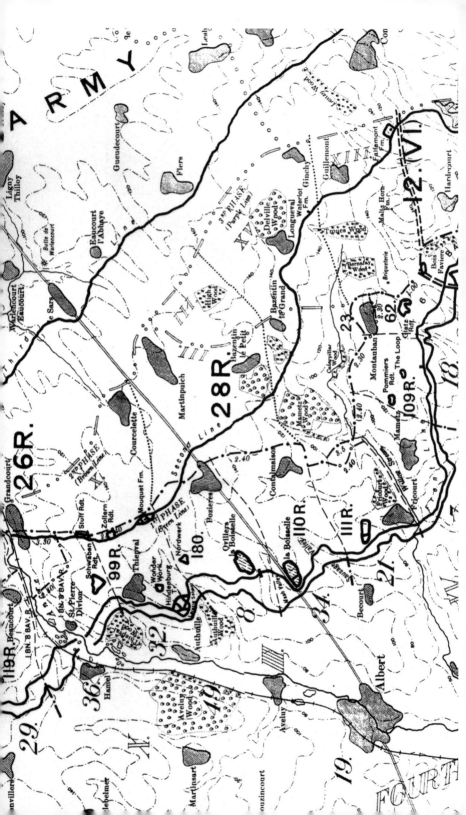

attacked by the 8th Division their second objectives ran from just south of Mouquet Farm and west of Pozieres village. The 34th Division's second objective was Contalmaison Wood and the western fringe of Contalmaison. The final or third objective which would be reached after two hours and forty minutes of fighting would include almost all of Pozieres village, the whole of Contalmaison and Acid Drop Copse, 300 metres east of Contalmaison communal cemetery.

The dispositions of the British troops who were designated to make the attacks upon those German troops in Ovillers and La Boisselle were as follows.

On the left of III Corps' front the attack would be made by the 8th Division and the bulk of all three of its brigades, the 70th, 25th and 23rd, would be placed in the front lines to effect the assault. The troops in the last two mentioned brigades, the 23rd and 25th were regular soldiers[8]. On the extreme right of that division's frontage Lieutenant Colonel Sandys' 2nd Middlesex would have the widest part of No Man's Land to cover, the gap between the trenches being more than 700 metres from the Middlesex positions towards the German lines, in Mash Valley, between Ovillers and La Boisselle. Next to the Middlesex men the 20th Northumberland Fusiliers, on the extreme left of the 34th Division's frontage, would share that same dismal prospect as they attacked towards the German trenches north of La Boisselle and on across the Albert – Bapaume road. The most advantageous position was that of the men instructed to make the direct attack upon Ovillers. These were the 2nd Royal Berkshires and 2nd Lincolns of 25 Brigade. Their attacks would be out of sight of the German defenders in the village on the eastern side of the spur until the last three or four hundred yards. North of Ovillers the position was very worrying to the 8th Division's commanding officer, Major General H.Hudson, who knew that his men would be overlooked from the immensely strong Leipzig Redoubt positions south west of Thiepval. So worried was Hudson that he had requested that his men be allowed to delay their attack until after the 32nd Division's assault on Thiepval, in order to ensure that any enfilade fire from Leipzig was suppressed. This proposal was overruled by Fourth Army.

III Corps' right assault division was therefore the 34th. This division was entirely comprised of New Army soldiers, Kitchener's men[9]. Two of the division's brigades were drawn largely from the heavily industrialised surroundings of Newcastle-upon-Tyne. On the left of the divisional front the Tyneside Scottish Brigade (102) would lead the attack astride the La Boisselle salient. The tip of that salient containing the village itself was not to be attacked directly, but rather pinched out

Shelling of the German trenches during the last week of June 1916 prior to the infantry assault at 7.30, Saturday, 1 July.

by attacks either side, culminating in the entry of bombing parties into the village. These small bombing parties would be supported by Lewis Gun teams and Stokes Mortars which would continue firing on the village, after the main barrage had lifted forward, until the bombing parties were ready to enter. In order to prevent any subsequent break out of Germans, C Company of the 18th Northumberland Fusiliers wasplaced in the British lines directly in front of the Glory Hole. This company were not to take any direct part in the assault. On the right of the 34th Division the men of 101 Brigade would make their attack across the wider expanse of No Man's Land in front of Heligoland. In immediate support of the two assault brigades the Tyneside Irish (103) Brigade would pass through, on having reached the second objectives, to make an advance towards Contalmaison and Contalmaison Wood. It is therefore easy to visualise the 34th Division's assault as being made in four columns, each column being three battalions in depth, each column having a frontage of approximately 400 metres.

To suppress fire from the Heligoland (Sausage Redoubt) positions a Trench Mortar position was dug, the night before the assault in No Man's Land. On the morning of 1st July, although its fire initially proved effective, the Stokes gun's position was clearly visible and it was subject to a counter bombardment which killed or wounded the whole crew, putting the gun out of action.

In support of the two assault divisions III Corps had command of the 19th (Western) Division, often referred to as the Butterfly Division. It was anticipated that during the assaults on Ovillers and La Boisselle the two leading brigades of the 19th Division would be brought up to the Tara – Usna positions [10] to take advantage of advances made by the 8th and 34th divisions. During the preliminary artillery bombardment of the German positions the 19th Division's guns operated alongside the guns of the other two divisions.

Unfortunately the secrecy of the assaults, both here and elsewhere along the British frontage, was compromised by the work of the Moritz

listening post, located just south of La Boisselle. This post reported to 56th Reserve Brigade HQ in Contalmaison that part of an order issued to the British 34th Division had been overheard. Its German translation read: 'The infantry must hold on obstinately to every yard of ground that is gained. Behind it is an excellent artillery.' Whilst this is not a particularly accurate translation of Fourth Army's words of encouragement issued to III Corps, it did reveal the essence of what was about to happen.

The assault made on La Boisselle and Ovillers on the morning of 1st July:

I have described these events in a series of snapshots, starting on the left of III Corps' front and moving towards the right and its junction with XV Corps. As we have noted, the assault would be undertaken by 34 Division on the right, consisting of 101, 102 and 103 Brigades, with the 8th Division on its left made up of the 23, 25 and 70 Brigades. The 19th Division was arranged in corps reserve, although its artillery units were already in action under the direct control of the other two divisions. The two large mines which were detonated two minutes before zero, at Lochnagar and Y Sap, had been driven forward using tunnels approximately 4'6" by 2'6" which had progressed at little more than ten feet a week throughout the preceding months. Their detonation was designed to disrupt the flanks of La Boisselle, throwing up 'lips' whose height would prevent enfilade machine gun fire across No Man's Land either side of the village salient.

All along the 8th Division's frontage the final intensification of the barrage from 7.22 onwards, supplemented by the fire of three Stokes Mortar sections (12 3-inch guns) behind each brigade, marked the opportunity for men to move out into No Man's Land. The leading waves moved forwards two to three hundred yards, but throughout it was apparent that the machine gunners in Ovillers were not subdued and at least two guns constantly swept the area of No Man's Land north of La Boisselle. Some way to their right the detonation of the mines at

41

La Boisselle, at 7.28 am, created both a spectacular outburst of flame and a gigantic plume of debris which gushed skywards in the most devastating and awesome cacophony of sound and shockwaves yet heard in warfare. 2nd Lieutenant C.A.Lewis of 3 Squadron RFC was flying overhead.

'The whole earth heaved and flashed, a tremendous and magnificent column rose up into the sky. There was an ear-splitting roar, drowning all the guns, flinging the machine sideways in the repercussing air. The earth column rose higher and higher to almost 4,000 feet. There it hung, or seemed to hang, for a moment in the air, like the silhouette of some great cypress tree, then fell away in a widening cone of dust and debris. A moment later came the second mine. Again a roar, the upflung machine, the strange giant silhouette invading the sky. Then the dust cleared and we saw the two white eyes of the craters.'[11]

Although quoted many times since, 2nd Lieutenant Lewis's words are so evocative that they have to be used to illustrate the power and enormity of what happened here eighty years and more ago. Although one of the 'eyes' is now closed it is impossible to stand on the lip of Lochnagar and not shudder at the sound of the airman's words, written in awe so long since. In the trenches below the shockwaves were severe enough to fracture stout soldier's legs braced apprehensively against the walls of the British trenches 250 metres distant, lower down Chapes Spur. German accounts described an event where 'stones rained down for a full minute striking the entire regimental sector.'! The detonation under the *Schwabenhohe* cost the 7th Company of RIR 110 more than half its men.

The wreckage of La Boisselle, seen across the gaping jaws of Y Sap crater. [Reed]

Fortified then by the sight of La Boisselle's seeming eclipse on their right, the 8th Division's men began to pour forward. Initially, at 7.30, that advance of the three brigades was carried out 'with great coolness and precision, and in excellent order'. Yet the sky overhead was soon blotched with the dull glare of red rockets, the German infantry's signal to their artillery to begin the deadly defensive barrage on No Man's Land. Within minutes, as the British waves neared the German front lines, the strength of that devastating barrage, and its accompanying incessant machine gun fire, rose to unprecedented levels of intensity. In the face of this terrifying weight of metal many of the men began to rush forward and bunch together where their proximity made them even more inviting targets.

1) 70 Brigade at the Nab facing the Nordwerk

This attack has to be seen in the context of its being overlooked on its left flank by Thiepval. It is best visualised on the road leading away from The Nab towards Ovillers, along which the complete and utter dominance of the Thiepval defences can be easily understood.

Initially 70 Brigade's attack, forming the left of the 8th Division's frontage, had some success since the early assaults on the western side of Leipzig Redoubt, by 32nd Division, diverted the attention of that position's defenders. The soldiers of the 8th KOYLI and 8th York & Lancs got across No Man's Land and into the first three lines of German trenches west of the Nordwerk. Unfortunately mounting casualties lessened the momentum of that advance and the Nordwerk itself and the trenches north east of The Nab were not taken. The 9th York & Lancs, in immediate support, were then cut down the instant they left their front lines by the ever increasing machine gun fire from Hindenburg trench, on Thiepval spur, and also from the southern face of Leipzig Redoubt which was not under direct attack by 32nd Division. The brigade reserves, the 11th Sherwood Foresters, were then progressing forward up choked trenches and across a sea of casualties in No Man's Land. Predictably the Sherwood Foresters were also devastated in their attempts to cross to the isolated men now fighting alone in the trenches west of the Nordwerk. Indeed, it was apparent that parties of Germans were now re-occupying some of their own front line system. A small party of fifty bombers did attempt to get up to the head of Nab Valley under cover of the lane embankments there, but those men were checked by a German machine gun placed higher up the re-entrant. As the morning progressed it became impossible to communicate with the parties of men from 8th KOYLI and 8th York & Lancs and the inevitable German counter attacks began to close in and

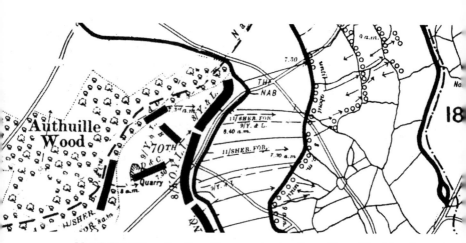

Map 5. Detail from the disposition map showing the position of British units north of the Albert – Bapaume road in 70 Brigade's area at zero hour on 1st July

surround these men.

By evening the whole of the positions attacked by 70 Brigade were back in German control. Casualties in the brigade were devastating, nearly 2,000 soldiers. Almost every officer who had attacked with the first two assault battalions had become a casualty including all four battalion commanding officers, Lieutenant Colonels Addison and Maddison being killed and the other two COs, Lieutenant Colonel Watson and Captain Poyser[12] being wounded.

Over five hundred of the men in each of those two leading battalions

Looking northwards towards Thiepval from the the area of the Nordwerk on Ovillers ridge. The trees on the left horizon mark the site of Leipzig Redoubt. Clearly visible is the Memorial to the Missing. In the middle distance are trees within the upper reaches of Blighty Valley.

The trees at Leipzig Redoubt   Memorial to the Missing at Thiepval

had also fallen. The casualties amongst the 9th York & Lancs and 11th Sherwood Foresters were hardly less severe. It was clear that, until Thiepval and Ovillers were captured, there was no chance of a successful infantry attack from The Nab positions. The failure of 70 Brigade here had produced catastrophic consequences for the men of 32nd Division. Amongst that division's units the 1st Dorsets, the 11th Borders 'Lonsdale' battalion and the 19th Lancashire Fusiliers (the 3rd Salford Pals) suffered terrible casualties from the machine guns firing from the Nordwerk across their brave but ill advised attempt to advance towards Mouquet Farm over the north western side of Blighty (or Nab) Valley.

2) 25 Brigade facing Ovillers

This attack is best visualised from the highest point along the road from The Nab leading into Ovillers. Here there are magnificent views over the surrounding countryside.

25 Brigade was estimated to have been presented with the easiest, if that can be the correct word, of the 8th Division's targets at Ovillers. Yet by comparison with the New Army's men of 70 Brigade the 25th Brigade was impotent to cope with the terrible intensity of rifle and machine gun fire emanating from the Ovillers' defences. The 2nd Royal Berkshires were unable to make progress. To their north, initially moving in lines but then progressing by short rushes from shell-hole to shell-hole, men of the 2nd Lincolns gained the German front line, north west of Ovillers, at 7.50 am. Small parties then pressed on towards the second trench from where they were eventually compelled to withdraw in the face of counter attacks by bombers and persistent enfilade fire from both flanks. The 70 or so remaining men who had survived 25 Brigade's attack were organised in the defence of these German front lines west of Ovillers by Lieutenant Colonel Reginald Bastard of the 2nd Lincolnshires. The Lieutenant Colonel was now commanding the remnants of three battalions and he was determined to continue the attack if support came. Calmly and professionally, on each flank, he ordered men to block the trenches with barbed wire as well as organising searches for uncleared dug-outs and any remaining stocks of German grenades. Here they held on for more than ninety minutes until driven out by counter attacks as their supplies of ammunition ran low. As they staggered back into the shelter of shell holes in No Man's Land they came across the remains of their support waves, hundreds of dead and dying men. The 1st Royal Irish Rifles, in immediate support, had been decimated by the German barrage as they had attempted to cross and leave the British trenches, only ten men having got over to join the

The view across Ovillers from a position east of La Boisselle. The British Military Cemetery is located in No Man's Land to the west of Ovillers village and the chalk marks left by German trenches which ringed the village can still be clearly seen

parties within the German trenches opposite. The 2nd Rifle Brigade were held in reserve at Donnet Post.

Reginald Bastard now ordered his remaining men to hold fast outside the German wire. Risking all he then ran back into the British trenches only to discover that the fourth battalion, from whom he had expected support, had been ordered not to go over. Nevertheless, fired with determination, he then collected all the stragglers from the three battalions which had attacked and ordered them to go over again, with

him, to reinforce the group left in front of the German wire. This party was immediately savaged by accurate rifle and machine gun fire as soon as they left the British lines and Reginald Bastard was forced to admit defeat in the face of untenable casualties. In view of the prominent role that his duties of leadership gave him, Reginald Bastard had indeed been fortunate to survive these events.

The casualties amongst the officers and men of 25 Brigade were not quite as heavy as those suffered by 70 Brigade. Nevertheless, more than 1,300 men fell here. Within the Berkshire battalion the casualties were 27 officers and 347 men, in the Lincolns 21 officers and 450 men. The 1st Royal Irish Rifles suffered 17 officer casualties and a further 429

Lieutenant Colonel Reginald Bastard, 2nd Lincolns.

among the men. The 2nd Rifle Brigade casualties were rather less severe, being only 4 officers and 115 men. Those few men who had survived unscathed lay scattered around the German lines in shell-holes all day. It was only at nightfall that these men were able to make their way back into the British lines.

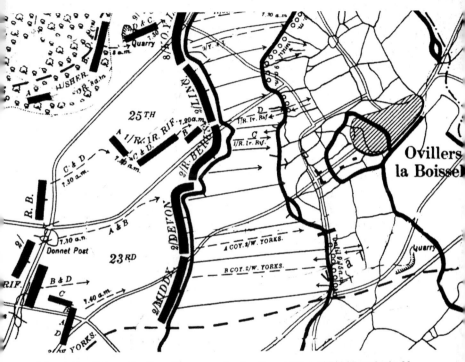

Map 6. Detail from the disposition map showing the position of British units in 23 and 25 Brigade's area facing Ovillers at zero hour on 1st July.

3) 23 Brigade south-west of Ovillers facing Mash Valley

The events which occurred here during the early hours of 1st July 1916 can best be visualised from the road leading from Ovillers towards La Boisselle, just south of the present day Ovillers communal cemetery, as it begins its descent into the upper confines of the Mash Valley re-entrant.

This brigade was allotted the unenviable task of crossing the northern confines of Mash Valley, on the north-western side of the La Boisselle salient. Here the land was utterly devoid of cover except for the shell holes and weed infested corn which formed the unreal landscape. It was anticipated that the brigade would be able to gain the

47

Albert-Bapaume road, in the region of the quarry between La Boisselle and Ovillers, and thereafter make use of the road in giving direction to its advance towards the western side of Pozieres village, its final objective.

As events turned out only small parties of men from the two leading battalions, the 2nd Middlesex and 2nd Devons, passed through the German front line in Mash Valley. A handful of men managed further progress but were stopped by the intensity of machine gun and rifle fire from their flanks. Lieutenant Colonel Sandys' worst fears had come to pass. The casualties amongst the 2nd Middlesex battalion were 22 officers and 601 men, whilst the 2nd Devons suffered 17 officer casualties and 433 amongst the men. The 2nd West Yorks lost 8 officers and 421 men in their attempts to cross No Man's Land here and the 2nd Scottish Rifles were therefore, mercifully, ordered to abort their advance.

The total casualties suffered by the 8th Division in front of Ovillers on this day were 5,121, including more than 1,900 men and officers killed and over 3,000 wounded. These figures included seven of the Division's Battalion COs[13]. The 180th Regiment, defending Ovillers opposite the 8th Division, had lost 78 killed and 124 wounded during the British preliminary bombardment. The defence of Ovillers on 1st July was undertaken by just two battalions of the 180th Regiment, their total casualties being just 4 officers and 79 men killed along with 3 officers and 181 men killed and 13 missing. The stark contrast in the experience of the opposing sides could not have been clearer, especially to the British Tommies who suffered so much with so little complaint.

However, further south at La Boisselle the carnage was worse, the consequences even more unbearable for the communities which raised the battalions whose task it was to capture that village.

That assault, made by the 34th Division on La Boisselle, has attained a terrible infamy within the chronicles of the British Army. In the context of the Great War many events became notorious as a consequence of the casualties which seemed, unendingly, to be produced over many weeks or months of campaigning. But La Boisselle attained its place in the war's legend because of the terrible concentration of killing which took place within minutes of the assault being launched here on the morning of 1st July 1916. And because of its position astride the Albert Bapaume road the story's bones are often the first ones to be heard and pondered by the many visitors who pass through the tranquillity of present day La Boisselle[14].

On the morning of 1st July 1916 the German troops who stood opposite the 34th Division were the 110th Reserve Regiment. As with

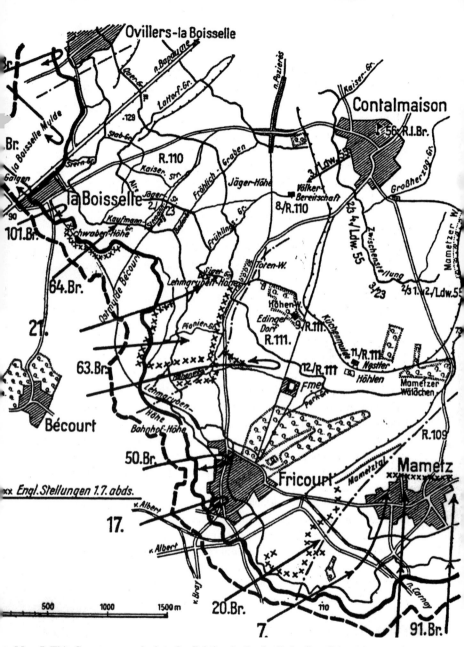

Map 7. This German map depicts the fighting in the La Boisselle - Fricourt area during the 1st July 1916. Whilst adding relatively little to the comparable British Official History's version of events it does suggest that little importance was attached to the penetration of small parties of British troops towards Contalmaison that day. Whilst the identification of the German unit's locations is reliable the suggested positions of the British units in front of La Boisselle are somewhat misleading.

The Albert - Bapaume road outside La Boisselle. This view looks south-westwards towards Albert from near the site of the British front lines. On the right of the road is Usna Hill, on the left is Tara Hill.

the 180th, at the village of Ovillers, the 110th's front lines were held by two of the regiment's battalions with a third in the intermediate and main Second Position. Again the depth of their bunkers had defied the British artillery's efforts to eradicate any possibility of organised defence and, once the attack was imminent, the 110th's riflemen and machine gunners lost no time in organising a rough firing line, certainly well in advance of the arrival of the first British soldiers on the German side of No Man's Land.

The plan being followed by the 34th Division was to employ all of the division's twelve battalions in the initial assault. They would attack in four columns, each column three battalions in depth with a frontage of four hundred yards. The first objective would be taken by the leading Brigade's assault battalions whose supports would take the second objective. These supports would then be leapfrogged by the Tyneside Irish whose objectives were just east of Contalmaison and south east of Pozieres. Astride the Albert – Bapaume road there was a gap, held by C Company of the 18th Northumberland Fusiliers, the Division's pioneer battalion, either side of which the two left hand columns of the division would pass, later dispatching special bombing parties into the confines of La Boisselle to clear it of any remaining defenders. The reality of the attack was one of terrible misfortune and the seeming inevitability of chaos. As the German machine guns behind La Boisselle came into action, sweeping No Man's Land and the forward face of the Tara –

Usna slopes, the front battalions of each column slowed and the front platoons of each succeeding wave became intermingled with their predecessors, forming large clusters of uncertain soldiers whose close concentration made them easy prey for the gunners opposite.

4) The Tyneside Scottish (102) Brigade at La Boisselle

102 Brigade was divided into two columns, the supporting battalion of each column having been 'borrowed' from 103 Brigade, the Tyneside Irish.

The best location from which to visualise the attack across Mash Valley, by the left column of 102 Brigade, is from the La Boisselle to Aveluy road where Keats Redan on the British front line was located. This position is to be found three hundred yards north west of the present day village cemetery.

The left column was led by the 1st and 4th Tyneside Scottish (20th and 23rd Northumberland Fusiliers) with the 2nd Tyneside Irish (25th Northumberland Fusiliers) in support. The 1st Tyneside Scottish were arranged to the north of Keats Redan whilst the 4th Tyneside Scots were south of Keats Redan facing Y Sap. North west of La Boisselle No Man's Land in the confines of Mash Valley is more than 700 yards wide and success in crossing it was dependant upon the artillery bombardment having made La Boisselle's defence untenable,

Map 8. This shows the dispositions and subsequent attacks of 102 Brigade astride the La Boisselle salient on the morning of 1st July 1916.

This view of La Boisselle was taken on 3rd July 1916. In a number of publications it has been mistakenly captioned as 'Lochnagar Crater'. The truth is that the image shows the village as seen from the lower slopes of Usna Hill just behind the British positions looking across Mash Valley, from a position north west of the village looking towards the south east. The scene is therefore Y Sap crater. Beyond the crater British shells can be seen bursting around the area of Alte Jager Strasse. On the original it is also possible to make out the jaws of the Lochnagar Crater in the distance. IWM Q69

weakening German morale and resolve to such an extent that the defenders would capitulate and surrender freely. In the event this attack across the huge width of No Man's Land was utterly disastrous. Even the successful detonation of Y Sap mine made little impact upon the defenders' ability to resist and very few Tynesiders made it across the vast empty wastes of Mash Valley below Y Sap's gleaming desolation. The 23rd Northumberland Fusiliers' War Diary recorded that 'heavy casualties were at once incurred, many men of our first line even being hit whilst getting over our front line parapet. Each company was played over into No Man's Land by its piper who continued to play until either killed or wounded'[15]. Among those soldiers who had effected the deepest penetration the bodies of Lieutenant Colonels Lyle and Sillery were later found. It was said that these officers' greatest concerns had been to be allowed to take part in the attack amongst their men. Lyle was last seen walking, 'stick in hand', about two hundred yards from the German trenches. Behind the unearthly white wreckage of Y Sap, although the village was seemingly obliterated by a week of artillery bombardment, the subterranean defences were intact and the defenders' morale surprisingly resilient. Even a British trench mortar bombardment of the village, maintained for twelve minutes after zero, failed to keep the men of 110th Regiment underground and their defence of this front line village has to be regarded as a remarkable feat of arms and determination. By evening no foothold had been gained in any German trench on the north western flank of the La Boisselle salient.

The postscript to these abortive attacks is recorded in the 4th Tyneside Scots War Diary. It is not hard to imagine the trying circumstances within which the Adjutant was attempting to record all that he had witnessed in these hours. But what also comes through is the complete lack of bitterness and a willingness to carry on in the best tradition of maintaining the men's spirits.

'Our stretcher bearers were conspicuous by their daring in bringing in wounded men in daylight under fire. The dressing station and the trenches near were soon congested with casualties and only by continual and very exhausting work by Captain J.N. Muirhead, our Medical Officer, and his staff were they able to gradually relieve this pressure, which was not until the following day. At 9 o'clock in the morning after all the men in the Battalion had been collected they were formed up behind the Usna-Tara line for a roll call to be taken and only about 100 men answered their names. During the course of the day about 20 men turned up. All the men were sent into dugouts to rest until the evening when they were formed up into parties for carrying rations and ammunition to our attacking troops. The only two officers who turned up for the roll call were Lt G.Shelson and 2/Lt C.Daggett who were very exhausted and had had a most harrowing time. From them it was learned of the gallant and unflinching way in which all our officers, N.C.O.s and men went over in this great attack without the slightest hesitation. .... Major MacIntosh and Captain Whitehead were seen by a few officers being carried out and although badly wounded were in excellent spirits and both expressed the wish to be back with the Battalion again soon. The Brigadier was delighted with the fine performance and bravery shown by the Battalion.'

But how the men felt, in the quiet darkness of their recollections, it is impossible to imagine.

The best vantage point to help you visualise the attack of 102 Brigade's right column is along the lane leading from La Boisselle to Lochnagar crater. As you approach the lips of the crater from the

The Tyneside Scottish coat of arms on the memorial seat at La Boisselle.

direction of La Boisselle the last three hundred yards are the site of *Schwaben Hohe*. Three hundred yards north east of *Schwaben Hohe*, looking past Contalmaison towards Pozieres, is *Kaufmann Graben* (trench).

102 Brigade's right column, consisting of the 2nd and 3rd Tyneside Scottish with the 3rd Tyneside Irish in support (21st, 22nd and 26th Northumberland Fusiliers), was faced with a rather less daunting width of No Man's Land to cross. This column made some startling advances, capitalising upon the defender's shock following the twin mines' detonation. Unfortunately relatively little of this advance could be held by the thinly scattered groups of men who were brave enough to advance so far. Starting as soon as the great Lochnagar mine was detonated on their right the men soon overran the *Schwaben Hohe* trenches north west of the mine and south of the village. Parties of men from the leading lines then crossed the next two lines of trenches including *Kaufmann Graben* and *Alte Jager Strasse*, close to Gordon Dump cemetery, gradually being thinned in number until a mere handful of men penetrated past Wold Redoubt on the La Boisselle – Contalmaison road as far forward as Bailiff Wood, only 500 yards from Contalmaison. Following a succession of German counter attacks the Tyneside Scots here withdrew to the confines of the *Kaufmann Graben* where they held and consolidated their gains. This consolidation was undertaken by seven officers and perhaps 200 men who had survived as an organised force from the original attack. The senior officer among this contingent was Major Acklom of the 22nd Northumberland Fusiliers.

About 100 metres south of Major Acklom's position, the rim of Lochnagar crater provided shelter for other parties of men. These included soldiers belonging to the 10th Lincolns, under command of the wounded 2nd Lieutenant Turnbull, as well as men belonging to both 102 and 103 Brigades. Lieutenant Colonel Howard of 24th Northumberland Fusiliers was brought into this position and died here, later that night, of his wounds.

5) 101 Brigade at Heligoland (Sausage Redoubt)

The scene of these events can best be visualised from the lane running down into Sausage Valley south east of Lochnagar crater. Here, within the valley, No Man's Land was sometimes more than 500 yards in width and the lane bisects the two opposing front lines. The high

Scots Redoubt   Round Wood   The Willow Patch   The rim of Lochnagar Crater

Sausage Valley

The view across Sausage Valley towards Bloater trench and Heligoland from the lane at the side of Lochnagar crater. On the horizon Round Wood and the Willow Patch can be seen clearly.

ground to the east of Sausage Valley is the Fricourt spur where Scots Redoubt stood, between the Heligoland front line trenches and an important second line known as Horseshoe Trench.

On the right hand side of the 34th Division's frontage two columns were formed by the battalions under command of 101 Brigade. Each of these two columns had one battalion to lead the assault, one in support together with a third battalion, drawn from 103 Brigade, in the rear. The left column consisted of the 10th Lincolns (the Grimsby Chums) with the 11th Suffolks in support. This column was expected to advance past the south eastern lip of the crater towards Bloater Trench which lay further up the Sausage Valley re-entrant. There was, therefore, a gap of some two hundred yards between this column and the right column of 102 Brigade which was to attack on the north western side of the crater. To compound the difficulties faced by the 10th Lincolns they were ordered to delay their assault until five minutes after the blowing of the mine, in order to reduce casualties from falling debris. The men were further hampered by the need to assemble behind their front line positions, again in order to minimise any casualties from falling debris. As events transpired this decision was naive and erroneous since the re-entrant formed by Sausage valley between *Schwaben Hohe* and Heligoland proved to be a terrible killing ground within which the 110th Reserve Regiment's machine gunners mowed down the brave but uncertain Tommies of 101 Brigade's left column.

The assault battalion of 101 Brigade's right column was the 15th Royal Scots, with that regiment's 16th Battalion in support. This column would advance towards the Heligoland position above the

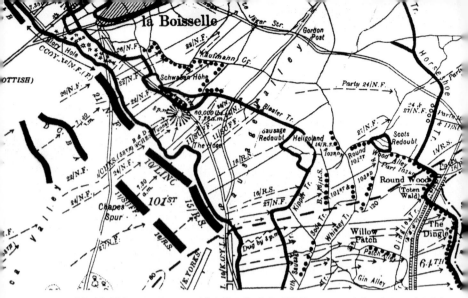

Map 9. This map shows another detail of the III Corps scene of action on 1st July, showing the dispositions and subsequent attacks of 101 Brigade across Sausage Valley towards Heligoland and Scots Redoubt.

eastern slopes of Sausage Valley and thence on towards Scots Redoubt. Below Heligoland No Man's Land was at its widest in this immediate area and the Scots would have to cross 600 yards of exposed ground before reaching the German front position standing on the commanding ground astride the western slopes of the Fricourt spur. In order to minimise the chances of grave losses the 15th Royal Scots had moved forwards to within 200 yards of the German positions during the final bombardment.

However, the delay in launching the left column meant that the German defenders had ample time to man their positions within Bloater Trench and Heligoland. The British barrage had already lifted when the Grimsby Chums began to clamber from their own trenches, with the Suffolks already close behind them on the lower slopes of Chapes Spur. However, these men were already under fire in enfilade from machine guns operating in Heligoland and from trenches at the head of Sausage Valley and also from positions to the rear of La Boisselle. Small numbers of the Grimsby men managed to make their way towards the vast crater's lip whilst tiny groups of the Suffolk soldiers crossed the lowest confines of Sausage Valley and entered Bloater Trench opposite. One terrible incident of note was the subsequent attempt by some men belonging to the 11th Suffolks who tried to fight their way into the Heligoland (Sausage Redoubt) positions but were burnt to death by flame-throwers as they reached the parapet there. During these events the Grimsby Chums lost 15 officers and 462 men whilst the Suffolks casualties amounted to 15 officers and 512 men. In view of these catastrophic events, along the lane south east of Lochnagar crater, the 24th Northumberland Fusiliers were ordered to halt in the British front line trenches. However, some of these men had already started forward and, as we shall see, were destined to make one of the most incredible, almost inexplicable, advances of any British unit on the morning of 1st July 1916. The remaining men of 101 Brigade's left column were forced to lie out in No Man's Land, throughout the day, unable to move for fear of the sweeping machine gun fire which still emanated from the Heligoland positions above and to their right. The reasons for the Heligoland's seeming invincibility are to be found in the right column's failure to maintain its anticipated direction.

The attacks made by the two Royal Scots battalions achieved a substantial advance past Round Wood and towards Peake Woods on the Fricourt to Contalmaison road. Unfortunately that advance was undertaken in an easterly direction, rather than the north easterly one which had been planned. The reason was the terrible weight of machine gun fire coming from the upper reaches of Sausage Valley and also from La Boisselle, causing havoc amongst the left platoons, especially those of the 16th Royal Scots. Progressively the men of the 15th and 16th Royal Scots were bunched together, instinctively veering right, away from the hail of bullets striking men on their left. These Scotsmen were being pushed towards, and eventually within, the sphere of operations of XV Corps. Having crossed the Fricourt to Contalmaison road, just north of its sunken section adjacent to Round Wood, they reached Birch Tree Wood, by 8.15 am, where the Scots became intermingled with soldiers from the 21st Division! Regrettably the Royal Scots advance across the Fricourt spur had left both Heligoland and Scots Redoubt uncaptured, ensuring that the soldiers from Grimsby and Cambridge to their left would be exposed to an unremitting hail of machine gun fire.

In order to improve their position and rectify some of the difficulties created by their loss of direction the Royal Scots reorganised. Men belonging to the 15th Battalion began to move northwards along Birch Tree Trench towards Peake Woods whilst the remaining men of the 16th Battalion took positions in support along the lane north of Round Wood. In the face of German counter attacks these dispositions became untenable without any close support and the 15th Royal Scots withdrew towards Birch Tree and Shelter Woods whilst the 16th Battalion's men (along with parties from the 27th Northumberland Fusiliers and small groups from the 11th Suffolks) to the area of Round Wood. From here these bands of men were marshalled by a wounded captain of the 11th Suffolks who organised an attack on Scots Redoubt along Wood Alley.

The redoubt was captured in an almost undamaged condition and the later construction of a communication trench by men of the XV Corps, that evening, enabled water and ammunition to be brought up to the Royal Scots near Birch Tree and Round Woods.

Unfortunately the Heligoland (Sausage Redoubt) position could not be taken, even though some desperate attacks upon these positions were organised in the afternoon. At 1.00 pm the redoubt and its surrounding trenches were bombarded for almost two and a half hours after which it was to be attacked by two parties of bombers from the 21st Division, on its south side, and 34th Division from the direction of Lochnagar crater. The attacks proved inconclusive and Heligoland held firm, continuing to dominate the surrounding positions for the rest of the day. Only after dark were some of the surviving men of 101 Brigade, trapped in No Man's Land throughout the long and tortured daylight hours, able to get back to their own lines.

6) The advance of the Tyneside Irish (103) Brigade

Technically this was the support Brigade, charged with taking the third objectives after the first two had been captured by the soldiers of 101 and 102 Brigades. In reality all of 34th Division's three brigades were launched into the attack simultaneously. Thereafter, little coherent evidence can be pieced together of the events which surround the destruction of this brigade of soldiers. Their commanding officer, Brigadier General N.J.G.Cameron, was out of action by 7.50 am, wounded by a machine gun bullet as he peered forward from his observation post on the Tara-Usna lines. Cameron was replaced in command by Lieutenant Colonel Steward of the 27th Northumberland Fusiliers, but that position proved an impossible one to fill. Already Steward's predecessor had witnessed the tragic and pointless exhibition of bravery as the battalions had swept down the forward slopes in front of La Boisselle. He had seen his men becoming hopelessly compressed

The Tyneside Irish coat of arms on the memorial seat at La Boisselle.

against the rearmost and struggling platoons of the Tyneside Scots. There must have been tears in his eyes as he realised, knowing there was nothing which could be done, that the targets this great mass of men presented to the German gunners were leading, inexorably, to carnage.

From that moment on the story is one of isolated bands, some moving on Contalmaison and later taking part in the defence of Shelter Wood and the fighting around Scots Redoubt. Other small groups fought with Major Acklom in *Alte Jager Strasse* falling back on *Kaufmann Graben* south of La Boisselle. By late evening three officers and about 80 men belonging to the 25th Northumberland Fusiliers were back in the British lines at Keats Redan, just north of the Albert – Bapaume road, having returned from their abortive attack across Mash Valley on the north side of La Boisselle. From right to left of the 34th Division's frontage it was apparent by nightfall that the Tyneside Irish and Scottish Brigades were little more than an utterly spent force. Rawlinson's decision to utilise the inflexible tactics of the parade ground in the Great Push had proven to be a catastrophic error of judgement, especially so here at La Boisselle and in front of Ovillers.

One of the most recognised of all photographs. This was taken just one minute after zero on the 1st July 1916 and shows a support company, belonging to one of the Tyneside Irish battalions, moving forward towards the highest ground on Tara Hill. The photograph was probably taken close to the Albert – Bapaume road near to trench map reference W.24.d. Within seconds of this scene being recorded many of these soldiers became casualties as they cleared the ridge and were exposed to the machine guns firing from positions within and to the rear of La Boisselle village. Notice soldiers carrying their rifles at the slope

1. Charles Douie, *The Weary Road*.
2. Charles Douie, *The Weary Road*.
3. Ernest Shephard, *A Sergeant-Major's War*.
4. Charles Douie, *The Weary Road*.
5. In total four mines were prepared to be blown at La Boisselle on the morning of 1st July. Apart from Lochnagar and Y Sap two further mines were made ready in front of Inch Street (X.19.b.9,5), each having been charged with only 8,000 pounds of ammonal.
6. Br Gen Trevor Ternan, *The Story of the Tyneside Scottish*, Northumberland Press. Date uncertain, 1920?
7. See Middlebrook, *First Day on the Somme*, pp 98-99.
8. The 8th Division, commanded by Major General H.Hudson, consisted of:
  22 Brigade:
      2nd Devonshire.
      2nd West Yorkshire.
      2nd Scottish Rifles.
      2nd Middlesex.
  25 Brigade:
      2nd Lincolnshire.
      2nd Royal Berkshire.
      1st Royal Irish Rifles.
      2nd Rifle Brigade.
  70 Brigade: (This Brigade had originally belonged to 23rd Division but had been exchanged with the 24 Brigade which was then sent to 'stiffen' another New Army division.)
      11th Sherwood Foresters.
      8th Kings Own Yorkshire Light Infantry.
      8th York and Lancaster.
      9th York and Lancaster.
  Pioneers: 22nd Durham Light Infantry.
9. The 34th Division, commanded by Major General E.C.Ingouville-Williams, consisted of:
  101 Brigade:
      15th Royal Scots (1st Edinburgh City).
      16th Royal Scots (2nd Edinburgh City).
      10th Lincolnshires (Grimsby Chums).
      11th Suffolk (Cambridge).
  102 Brigade:
      20th Northumberland Fusiliers (1st Tyneside Scottish).
      21st.Northumberland Fusiliers (2nd Tyneside Scottish).
      22nd Northumberland Fusiliers (3rd Tyneside Scottish).
      23rd Northumberland Fusiliers (4th Tyneside Scottish).
  103 Brigade:
      24th Northumberland Fusiliers (1st Tyneside Irish).
      25th Northumberland Fusiliers (2nd Tyneside Irish).
      26th Northumberland Fusiliers (3rd Tyneside Irish).
      27th Northumberland Fusiliers (4th Tyneside Irish).
  Pioneers: 18th Northumberland Fusiliers.
10. During the momentous events of this day one battalion of the 19th Division, 58 Brigade, the 9th Cheshires, was actually brought into the Lochnagar crater via the tunnel prepared by the miners of 179 Tunnelling Company. The tunnel had been cleared of debris and wounded by Lieutenant Nixon. The Cheshire's men were moved forward from their positions on Tara Hill at 7.00 pm.
11. C.A.Lewis, *Sagittarius Rising*.
12. Having come to the command of the 8th KOYLI because of the sickness of his senior officers prior to the battle. At this stage the strain on many older regulars, who had become COs of New Army battalions, was starting to show.
13. Lt.Col B.L. Maddison, 8th Yorks & Lancs, killed. Lt.Col A.J.B. Addison, 9th Yorks & Lancs, killed. Lt.Col A.M. Holdsworth, 2nd Royal Berks, DoW. Lt.Col C.C. Macnamara, 1st Royal Irish Rifles, DoW. Captain K.E. Poyser, 8th KOYLI, wounded. Lt.Col H.F. Watson, 11th Sherwood Foresters, wounded. Lt.Col E.T.F. Sandys, 2nd Middlesex, wounded and subsequently committed suicide.
14. The 34th Division lost seven of its battalion COs this day. These included all of the Tyneside Scottish Brigade's COs, Lt.Cols C.C.A. Sillery, F.C. Heneker, A.P.A. Elphinstone and W. Lyle, all killed. The CO of the 1st Tyneside Irish battalion, Lt.Col L.M. Howard was wounded on this day (later dying of those wounds) whilst Lt.Cols J.H.M. Arden of the 2nd Tyneside Irish and Lt.Col M.E. Richardson of the 3rd Tyneside Irish were wounded. 103 Brigade's CO, Brigadier General N.J.G. Cameron was also wounded.
15. PRO. WO95 2463.

Chapter Three

FURTHER EVENTS IN THE
OVILLERS–LA BOISSELLE–CONTALMAISON
AREA DURING THE SUMMER OF 1916

At 10.00 pm on the evening of 1st July 1916 General Rawlinson issued the orders by which the attack would be resumed the following day. The bulk of those orders dealt with the areas in the centre and left of the front where the attacks had failed on 1st July. As expected III Corps were ordered to capture La Boisselle and Fricourt, moving forward to take Contalmaison. However, there was to be no immediate exploitation of the advance on the right of the British front, adjacent to the French forces east of Montauban. In those areas, where some remarkable success had been achieved, an air of organised yet calm activity reigned throughout the 2nd July. Between Fricourt and Montauban British reinforcements and supplies were being moved across No Man's Land without artillery response.

By contrast, the situation at Ovillers-La Boisselle was a difficult one. A night attack had been planned in which two brigades of the 19th Division[1] would attack La Boisselle village at 10.30 pm, late on the 1st July. The attack was never made since neither 57 nor 58 Brigades' men could be got forward in time across the devastated ground littered with the bodies of the 34th Division's soldiers. Late that evening the communication trenches west of La Boisselle were still cluttered with the frantic movements of the stretcher bearers and the weary, cumbersome efforts of the walking wounded.

At Ovillers the situation was further complicated by the decision to relieve the 8th Division's infantry by the 12th Division, sent up from Army Reserve[2]. By an extraordinary feat of logistics the change-over was completed before dawn on the 2nd. A Forward Observation Officer of the RFA watched the departure of one unit which had suffered particularly heavily, the 2nd Middlesex. 'There was one officer and twenty eight men, all that remained of a very gallant battalion.'[3]

How those thousands of men in the 12th Division coped as they were brought up is difficult to imagine. In view of the grotesque numbers of casualties still being cleared the scene must have sparked a sense of utter dread as the men struggled forward in the blackness, only occasionally illuminated by the glow of flares and the flickering orange and steely blue hues of explosions. The 5th Berkshires' War Diary recorded that the 'trenches were found to be in a very filthy state, with many dead and wounded lying about'[4]. The grim stories of the soldiers they passed, en route to the shell torn front trenches, almost certainly filled each young man with foreboding. For the soldiers of the 12th Division that merciless night, as they marched up to Ovillers, would have seemed like an unending terror. Nevertheless, orders had been issued demanding that the 12th Division complete the capture of Ovillers that morning, following a dawn attack. The reality was that the newly arrived troops were in no position to undertake any offensive in front of Ovillers and the day was spent in familiarisation, recovery and the preparation required to dig new assembly trenches for forthcoming attacks. The unfortunate consequence was that the German companies within Ovillers' front line trenches were able to be relieved.

At La Boisselle the German accounts of the fighting here detail how, at dawn on the morning of 2nd July, the 9th Royal Welch Fusiliers and 6th Wiltshires made their first attacks on the village. During this fighting they were unable to make real progress against determined German defence led by Leutnant der Reserve Wirthwein and Hauptmann Heine. Nevertheless, during those attacks these two German officers were severely wounded and it became clear to the German command that their reserves at La Boisselle would soon be exhausted. The last of those reserves, belonging to III/R110 and detachments of 12/23 under the command of Leutnants der Reserve Hubner and Gach, were sent up, but the strength to resist was going. By this time arrangements were already in hand for 58 Brigade, of the 19th Division, to attack La Boisselle again at 4.00 pm. As a diversionary ruse Ovillers was bombarded from 3.30 until 4.00 pm. The ploy worked and, as the attack on La Boisselle began, the German artillery mistakenly put their defensive barrage around Ovillers allowing 58 Brigade's men an almost free run to the south. The attack was again made by the 6th Wiltshires and 9th Royal Welch Fusiliers, now aided on their right by the 9th Cheshires who emerged from the area of the crater at Lochnagar to attack towards the southern aspect of the village's defences. By late afternoon, after severe fighting, those remaining German troops in the *Kaufmann Graben* were forced back to the *Alte Jager Strasse*. Thus, by 9.00 pm these three British battalions had cleared the western part of the village as well as its southern defences, and had also consolidated their defensive positions along the lane just yards to the west of the church. In view of the catastrophic events of 1st July the success of these three battalions in capturing the larger part of La Boisselle was nothing short of a remarkable feat of endurance and bravery.

As a further demonstration of the ascendancy the Tommies were gaining at La Boisselle during the afternoon of 2nd July, more progress was made further south by two companies of the 7th East Lancs, of 56 Brigade, who captured the Heligoland (Sausage Redoubt) positions.

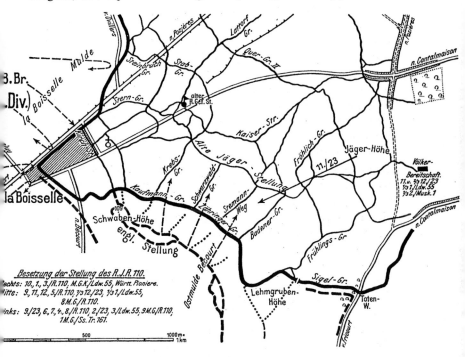

Map 10. La Boisselle 2.7.16 shows the German perspective on the fighting for that village on day two of the Somme Battle.

The events now hinged on the events of noon, 2nd July, when General Rawlinson had issued orders to X and VIII Corps to attack again, in the areas of Thiepval and Serre, whilst instructing III Corps to act in close co-operation by simultaneously taking Ovillers. This broad attack would commence at 3.15 am on the 3rd July following one hour's intensive bombardment. As matters evolved the left attack at Serre was reduced in importance, but the anticipation of combined attacks on Ovillers and Thiepval came to have a real bearing on future events. The problem, in essence, was that Rawlinson was reinforcing failure below the Thiepval – Pozieres ridge whilst neglecting success further south. It quickly became clear to Haig that Rawlinson's preparations for these attacks on 3rd July were drawing Fourth Army's attention away from exploiting the German's near collapse around Montauban and further east.

Military Cemetery   Ovillers Church

The site of the attack undertaken by the 5th Royal Berks, on the morning of 2nd July, along the lane leading towards Ovillers. This photograph was taken at the site of Argylle Street communication trench a little way behind the British front lines facing Ovillers village. (See Map 11.)

Unfortunately for the Tommies facing Ovillers, just twenty minutes before their attack was due, III Corps were informed by General Gough that his X Corps' attack could not be undertaken because of assembly delays. III Corps were therefore destined to attack on their own on a narrow front without flank protection. The outcome was drearily predictable. Nevertheless, the bombardment opened, spectacularly and optimistically, on time at 2.15 am, with Corps' artillery as well as batteries belonging to 12th Division and two brigades of the 19th Division's artillery. To improve the chance of success a number of new assembly trenches had been dug overnight, reducing the width of No Man's Land at its widest from 800 to 500 yards. The right of the attack against the south of Ovillers was undertaken by 35 Brigade, with the 5th Royal Berks and 7th Royal West Kents as the leading battalions. On their left, attacking the northern aspect of the village, was 37 Brigade using the 6th Queen's and 6th Royal West Kent as their assault battalions. Operation orders instructed the men to crawl forward into No Man's Land to 'within easy assaulting distance' during the final ten minutes of intensive bombardment. At the end of that bombardment the barrage would lift onto a line running through the church and thence, after a further 30 minutes, onto a line to the east of the village.

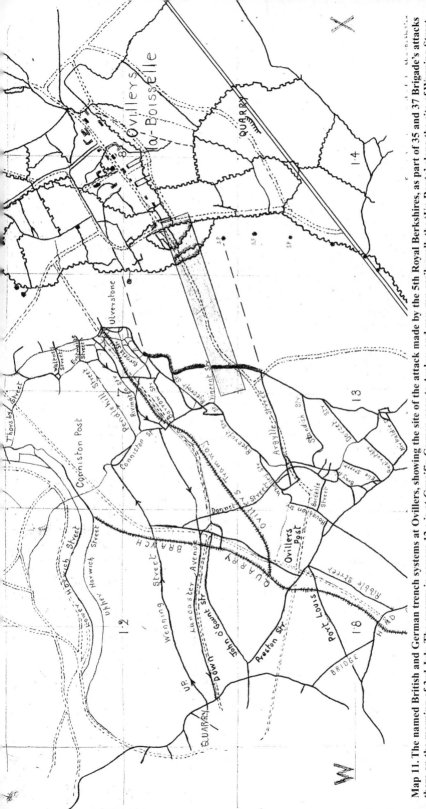

Map 11. The named British and German trench systems at Ovillers, showing the site of the attack made by the 5th Royal Berkshires, as part of 35 and 37 Brigade's attacks there on the morning of 3rd July. The quarry in square 12.c is at Crucifix Corner, near to Aveluy, and you can easily walk the 'Up Route' along the site of Wenning Street, towards where these men made their attacks. The map is based upon that found in the 5th Royal Berks' War Diary, PRO WO95 1850.

Even before the attack began, at 3.15 am, a sustained response from the German artillery had fallen heavily upon the British assembly, front line and communication trenches. But the eight waves of soldiers moving forward across No Man's Land were relatively free from that shelling and some had got sufficiently far forward before zero to be able to surprise many of the German front line defenders. Such timing was a classical use of the dawn attack, towards the as yet unrisen sun, making use of the half light to give direction to the attacking waves. Although faced by a great deal of enfilade machine gun fire from the La Boisselle flank and indirect fire from Thiepval area, as well as direct fire from behind Ovillers, these men pressed forward as best they could. In the frontage attacked by the Berkshires there were many gaps in the German wire although the shelling had also gouged deep shell holes which hugely impeded the progress of each man.

In the 6th Queens' attack their first platoons of B Company, on the Battalion's right, got to the German parapet but here the officer in charge was killed and the majority of the men hit by machine gun and rifle fire. Of the subsequent platoons almost all the men were wounded in attempting to cross No Man's Land. The first platoons of the left Company, C, lost direction and veered northwards into the Royal West Kent's attack. Their support platoons were devastated in No Man's Land as they searched for gaps in the German wire.

South of the 6th Queens the Berkshires seized the almost empty first lines of trenches with great verve. Maintaining their impetus the support positions on the outskirts of Ovillers were overrun and the Berkshires pressed towards 'Shrapnel Terrace', engaging in hand to fighting with the defenders. The Berkshires' War Diary is a vivid account, written by the battalion's commanding officer, detailing many of the trials which his men were exposed to in attempting an attack on a fortified village, and explaining that,

'many dugouts were bombed, and it became obvious that unless we could procure a plentiful supply of bombs, it would be impossible to hold on to what ground we had gained. It proved to be a very dark morning, and in the darkness it was extremely difficult to recognise friend from foe, or even the trenches themselves which had been considerably damaged by our shell fire, besides which, the noise of the bombardment which had now lifted to the northern outskirts of the village, and the fire of innumerable machine guns, was deafening, and made it quite impossible to hear orders given. ... The German dugouts appear to have been quite undamaged by the heavy bombardments, and as soon as we commenced to throw bombs down into them, the enemy swarmed out of entrances further along fully armed with bombs, so that there is no doubt that they were connected by some means underground. ... The Commanding officer and the Adjutant went forward shortly after the last wave had left, it was still quite dark, and impossible to discern faces 50 yards away. On reaching the German front line trenches about 100 men were found, between there and the second line. Considerable bombing was heard on the right and in front, and the enemy could be seen advancing from the left. There was much confusion in the darkness, and men from the 7th Suffolks and 9th Essex were seen to be mixed up with our own. The noise was deafening, and it was impossible to make oneself heard. The bulk of the men fell back to the German front line trench, some were inclined to go further, others stood on the top and appeared not to know what to do. Only one officer could be found in the locality (Captain Wace) and he was endeavouring to rally the men, and to get them to go forward.'

Although dawn had now broken it was still impossible for the British artillery observers to see through the swirling smoke and judge what was unfolding. The reality was a ceaseless wearing down of these attacking battalions. Although supported by two companies of the 6th Buffs, who had also got across early, the assault battalions' men in Ovillers village were now cut off. The German artillery barrage continued to pound the British lines, and intense machine gun fire now raked No Man's Land. It was impossible for any more of the 12th Division's support or reserve battalions to get across, although many had initially tried, bravely, to reach their comrades trapped in the warren of trenches in front of Ovillers.

'After a brief reconnaissance the Commanding officer decided that it would be quite impossible to retain our hold on the German front line trench which was almost entirely obliterated, and extremely deep, exposed as we were to an attack from both flanks, as well as from the front. It would have been impossible to have consolidated sufficiently in the time available, added to the fact that we should probably have had to remain there throughout the entire day quite unsupported, and entirely cut off, with no reserve of bombs or S.A.A. By this time the enemy had started a deadly cross fire with machine guns across No Man's Land, from the direction of X.14.a.3.5 and X.7.d.95.95., so the Commanding officer withdrew what men he could collect and made them dig in on the Albert – Ovillers Sunken Road facing south. This road afforded complete protection from the north, and was enfiladed from the East. About 80 – 100 men were dug in here, and remained there throughout the day, quite unmolested. They were withdrawn by order of the GOC as soon as it was dark. Lieutenant and Adjutant Gold was killed on this road, just behind the C.O.'[5]

Those few men who were left in the German trenches were now being hunted down mercilessly. They were exhausted physically and of ammunition, water and grenades. As early as 9.00 am the 12th Division reported total failure to their Corps command. In bald statistical terms the action in front of Ovillers on the morning of 3rd July cost 2,400 officers and men. In the late afternoon of the 3rd the Berkshires' War Diary records, in an unusually human and poignant manner, the meeting of those old friends who had survived.

'The Battalion which consisted of about 70 men, and the C.O., was ordered to go to the Albert defences for the night. Here the men made bivouac shelters, and the officers and N.C.O.s who had been left at the Transport lines rejoined, and cookers were brought up. In the evening 2nd Lieutenants Breach and May, and about 60 men who had been dug in in No Man's Land, rejoined. We were all very glad to see them.'

Captain Percy Wace, referred to in the diary above, died of his wounds this day.

However, our story can now switch back to La Boisselle where the 3rd July witnessed intense hand to hand fighting and the winning of two Victoria Crosses. These events had begun unexpectedly with the 9th Essex who had drifted away from the rest of 35 Brigade's attack at Ovillers and had blundered into a strong party of Germans just north of La Boisselle. These had been taken prisoner and handed over to the 19th Division's men. Even before the Essex men's intervention 57 Brigade of the 19th Division had been moved forward, on the left flank of 58 Brigade, in order to allow the simultaneous assault from north and south of the La Boisselle salient, at 3.15 am, which initially carried the village defences. Before that attack had been launched the 10th Worcester's commanding officer, Lieutenant-Colonel Royston-Piggott had made his way forward to the crater at Y Sap with his adjutant, Captain Gillum-Webb. Both men were shot here,

Royston-Piggott fatally through the heart. Nevertheless, from the north the attack was made by the 8th North Staffs with the now leaderless 10th Worcesters on their left. For some time after the start of this operation the men were unable to see each other and it was only after daybreak that the fighting reached its climax. During this period immediately after dawn a number of the Worcesters had fought their way clear of the eastern side of the village. Amongst these Worcesters was Lieutenant R.W. Jennings whose bombing party had penetrated to the German third line trenches. The British position was thus advanced by more than 400 yards and the men were able to marvel at the depth and condition of the labyrinthine German dugouts which had withstood all that had been thrown against them during the preceding ten days.

As soon as rockets were launched to indicate that La Boisselle had fallen a veritable rain of mortars and howitzer shells began to fall about the men. Within minutes the inevitable counter attack began, directed against 57 Brigade from the direction of Pozieres. Equally inevitably the supply of Mills bombs dwindled and the Germans began to infiltrate back into the houses at the eastern end of the village. In the midst of these events Lieutenant Jennings was badly wounded, his leg

This photograph shows men belonging to the 10th Worcesters escorting German prisoners from the La Boisselle battlefield on 3rd July.

shattered by machine gun fire, yet Private Turrall stayed behind. In truth there was little that Turrall could do. The other members of Lieutenant Jennings' party had all been killed by the burst of machine gun fire and he was now isolated in the German controlled portion of ground, north east of La Boisselle. The Worcester's regimental history records the scene[6].

'Private Turrall crawled to his wounded officer and dragged him slowly to shelter in a shell-hole. Then he set to bandaging the wound, using the haft of his entrenching tool as a splint, and binding it with one of his own puttees. As he worked, a bomb burst close to his head: then another. A German bombing party had seen him moving in the shell-hole. He picked up his rifle and opened fire on the bombers, who were working forward along a hedge. A gap in the hedge enabled him to shoot two of them: the others gave up the attack. Peering from the shell-hole he saw a wave of German infantry pouring forward from the east - a strong counter-attack. Resistance to such force was useless, but he did not think of surrender. The subaltern had fainted. Private Turrall flung himself flat and feigned death. He was prodded with bayonets and then left. The counter-attack then swept on to break against the Battalion in the village.'

The village of La Boisselle on 3rd July. This photograph [IWM Q68] is adjacent to, and on the left of, that which illustrated Y Sap in the previous chapter.

Later, as the fighting died away into the darkness that night Private Turrall saw his opportunity and dashed back, into the British lines, carrying Lieutenant Jennings on his back. Within a short while Thomas Turrall was back amongst his comrades in the thick of the fighting for La Boisselle. Unfortunately Lieutenant Jennings' wounds proved fatal and he died later that night, but not before dictating an account of Turrall's actions.

The fight was now very much a personal one, a matter of honour in which the bravery of an individual could lift the efforts of those who saw his actions. Certainly Private Turrall's efforts fall into that category and another such inspirational man was Lieutenant Colonel Carton de Wiart of the 8th Gloucesters, whose battalion along with the 10th Warwicks had been sent forward to reinforce the North Staffs and Worcesters after the most determined German counter-attacks began. Although handicapped by the loss of an eye in Somaliland, and a hand at Second Ypres, de Wiart was placed in command of the defence of La Boisselle by the Division's GOC, Major General G.T.M. Bridges, after his early morning reconnaissance into the village. Bridges' action was necessary since all the other commanding officers of the brigade had become casualties[7]. It was said of Adrian Carton de Wiart that whenever required he pulled the pins from his Mills grenades using his teeth, grimly determined to maintain his position at all costs. Those German counter attacks had forced the Wiltshires, Cheshires and 9th Welch Fusiliers of 58 Brigade to give ground back to their starting lines. Only the intervention of the 9th Welch had regained the position soon after midday. In the midst of these events 57 Brigade had also been counter-attacked in strength and it was during these long hours, between 11 am and late afternoon, that Adrian Carton de Wiart's inspirational example spurred his colleagues and men on.

Within the devastated confines of La Boisselle barely a brick has been left standing by the bombardments upon it fired by the artillery of both sides to the conflict here! This photograph shows men belonging to the 10th Worcesters deepening a trench.

By evening the German's counter-attacks were held, on a trench running through the ruins of the church, a gain over the previous day's position of 100 yards but far less than the 400 which had been achieved during the dawn attacks early that morning. Private John Price, 15797, of the 10th Worcesters was dead. Like many of the men who fought at La Boiselle his body was never recovered. He is commemorated on the Thiepval Memorial to the Missing (pier 5A/6C).

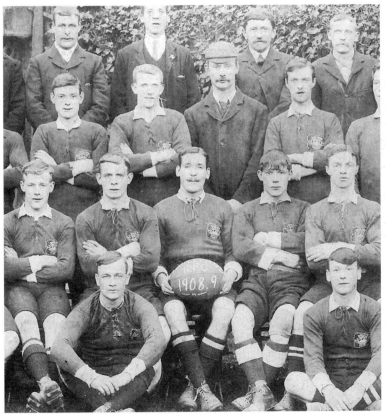

Private John Price's wife, Laurel. Laurel's experience of the Great War was one of terrible tragedy. Her two brothers were also killed, their names being recorded on the Menin Gate at Ypres. [Kean-Price]

Private John Price (holding the ball) with many of his friends from the Moreland's Excelsior Rugby Team, during the season of his captaincy, 1908-9. John Price's family suffered the tragedy of a double blow when, three days after John's death, his brother Walter was also killed, here at La Boiselle whilst serving with the 8th Gloucesters, another of the battalions in 57 Brigade. Like his brother, Walter is commemorated on the Thiepval Memorial. [Kean-Price]

Nightfall on the 3rd July saw the departure of the 34th Division from the area of La Boisselle. Since the arrival of the 19th Division the remnants of the 34th had been moved to the right, holding the ground on the south-east side of Sausage Valley around Scots Redoubt. As darkness fell the 23rd Division relieved the 34th, marking the end of what had become a nightmare for those men who had survived unscathed. The casualties of the 34th during the period 1st to the 5th July amounted to 6,811 of all ranks. On their arrival in reserve 102 and 103 Brigades from Newcastle-upon-Tyne were exchanged for the 111th and 112th from the 37th Division. The 34th was returned to its original constitution on 21st August after the processes of re-equipping and training the many replacement drafts had been completed.

The Position on the morning of 4th July

During the night of 3/4th July the weather began to turn sour again. The 10th Worcesters' War Diary recounts how, that morning,

'The Battalion withdrew to RYCROFT AVENUE after wandering some distance over the countryside endeavouring to find this trench. In the afternoon we were badly shelled, chiefly by 5.9 cm guns or higher. One shell obtained a direct hit on a party of men killing five and wounding two more. As always seems the case they were some of the best men in the Battalion. The mud in this trench was very bad and to make matters worse it rained hard for a couple of hours. At 9.00 pm the Battalion was ordered to move down to the old British front line. On arriving there by way of Andrews Avenue, which in places was up to the knees in water, we found the Staffordshire Regiment in possession. After frantic telephoning to Brigade we eventually fitted in on the left of Keats Redan in the old British lines where we spent a damp and miserable night.'[8]

Rain had fallen overnight and during the 4th July heavy showers turned into the saturating afternoon thunderstorm to which the Worcesters' diary refers. The trenches began to fill with water. The weight of traffic, here at La Boisselle, made movement in the clinging mud terribly slow. In front of Ovillers the military position was virtually unchanged from the situation before the 1st July. The trenches running almost due south from the tip of Authuille Wood, down to the Albert-Bapaume road, still formed the British front position. This sector was still under the control of the 12th Division opposite whom the Germans still controlled the whole of the Ovillers sector. However, from south of here onwards the position was new. The British front line now ran along the Albert-Bapaume road before turning south east through the eastern end of La

Boisselle where the 19th Division was still engaged. From here the lines ran in an east-south-easterly direction, past the southern end of Mametz Wood towards Bernafay Wood and the junction with the French Army. North of Fricourt, facing Contalmaison, were the 23rd Division, and on their right, also facing towards Contalmaison, were the 17th Division which included the 12th Manchesters in their ranks. For the moment, then, La Boisselle had become the fulcrum around which the British success adjacent to the French Army hinged.

This situation had been discussed at a Corps' Commanders conference on the afternoon of the 3rd. As a result of that meeting a Fourth Army order was issued at 9.45 pm that evening, detailing the nature of the forthcoming attacks to be undertaken by III Corps at Ovillers-La Boisselle, with XV Corps to their right at Mametz Wood and XIII Corps north of Montauban, further to their right. The order announced that every preparation would be made for a general attack on the German second position in the region of Longueval to Bazentin le Petit[9] and east of Pozieres. Within this context III Corps was to capture Contalmaison and control a line running from the north western tip of Mametz Wood, across Pearl Alley towards Contalmaison and thence westwards towards Ovillers. This would be undertaken on 7th July, on which date Mametz Wood, Trones Wood and Hardecourt would also be captured as necessary preliminaries to the attacks towards Longueval and Bazentin le Petit.

During the morning and early afternoon of the 4th July most of the remaining part of La Boisselle was captured. This action was begun at 8.30 am. The objective was to push the Germans back from the eastern boundaries of the village. On the right side of the attack, in and beyond the southern part of the village, was 56 Brigade. Here any advance across the open was impossible and the fight became a series of bombing exchanges, supported by Lewis gun fire and trench mortar fire, as the Tommies fought their way up a series of communication trenches and cleared the deep dugouts. On the left of 56 Brigade the 57th were fighting for the trench on the northern side of La Boisselle. Here the fighting was severe, the Germans employing hidden machine guns and the British determined to use the bayonet at every opportunity. The 19th Division's account of this fighting describes two extraordinary events. The first was the sight of a British Officer, bravely and almost unconcernedly walking with revolver in hand along the parapet of a trench, protecting his team of bombers who were advancing within its confines. The second was described as,

'A dramatic bombing duel between a British soldier and a German. Each combatant stood on the parapet of a trench, about twenty five yards apart, in full view. No one interfered or fired a shot at these gallant fellows but let them fight it out. They exchanged three throws each, but the last bomb thrown by the British soldier knocked the German out.'[10]

During the fighting involving this Brigade all four of its battalion commanders were either killed or wounded before the Brigade front was taken over by Lieutenant Colonel Winser, 7th South Lancs. By 2.30 pm the whole of the village bar a few ruins at its north-eastern tip were in British control[11] and some progress had also been made by bombers along the trench leading out towards Ovillers from the north of La Boisselle. Simultaneously some progress was made by bombing parties from the 17th Division along the trenches facing Contalmaison north of Shelter Wood.

In one of the very best of the portraits taken during the Great War two British soldiers give aid to two German POWs captured during the fighting around La Boisselle, probably photographed on 3/4th July.

The communal cemetery at La Boisselle, photographed soon after the German's departure on 4th July. [Reed]

As part of the continuing preparations for the attack on the main German Second position XV Corps was due to capture the southern portion of Mametz Wood first thing on 5th July. That attack took place at 12.45 am. Although not successful in gaining any of Mametz Wood these events did enable III Corps to improve its own position. From 4.00 am fighting became heavy in the area of Horseshoe Trench, 400 metres west of Peake Woods, as bombers of 69 Brigade edged slowly forwards. That attack was followed by a sustained infantry assault which had resulted in continuous and close quarter fighting in Horseshoe Trench. Unfortunately much of those gains were lost to a strong German counter attack at 10.00 am. During the afternoon the Germans continued to press forward hard in this area and the whole of 69 Brigade became engaged in the fighting.

The 23rd Division had therefore been fighting throughout the day. Nevertheless, at 6.00 pm, Brigadier General Lambert ordered an attack over the open ground and it was at this time, in the early evening, that 2nd Lieutenant Donald Simpson Bell, 9th Battalion Yorkshire Regiment, won his Victoria Cross whilst attacking a machine gun crew, along with Corporal Colwill and Private Batey. Subsequently the Horseshoe Trench position was retaken by 69 Brigade's men. Five days later Bell was destined to lose his life at Contalmaison when replicating this act of heroism during the course of his battalion's attack on that

British bombers are pictured advancing on 6th July along the floor of Avoca Valley towards La Boisselle from the direction of Becourt. The track is a river of mud and the men are keeping off it.

village on 10th July.

However at La Boisselle the position was static and any efforts to broaden the re-entrant east of the village met with no success. It was here, during the afternoon of the 5th, that Lieutenant Thomas Wilkinson of the 7th Loyal North Lancashires inspired all around him with his extraordinary bravery. Following an unplanned withdrawal by men of the 7th East Lancs Wilkinson saw that the East Lancs men had left a Lewis gun behind. It was already clear to Wilkinson that the withdrawal would risk losing much hard won ground and he rushed forward with two men, got the Lewis gun into action and held up the advancing Germans until a subsequent bayonet charge, by C Company of the 7th Loyal North Lancs, recovered the position. During a later bombing attack Lieutenant Wilkinson further distinguished himself by dispersing a group of German bombers, operating on the far side of a trench block, with a Lewis gun which he had brought into the open, quite unconcerned about his own safety. It was towards the close of this day's fighting that Lieutenant Wilkinson was killed. He had already attempted to bring in a badly wounded man, under heavy fire, when he was killed whilst making a second attempt to recover the man lying out in the open. Thomas Wilkinson thus became the third soldier serving

La Boisselle village

Chapes Spur

Avoca Valley today. On the right are the lower slopes of Chapes Spur across which communication trenches spread towards the British front lines west of Lochnagar crater.

with the 19th Division to win the Victoria Cross in this notorious village.

On the night of the 5th July the 12th Division's men took over in La Boisselle from the exhausted 57 Brigade[12]. The following day attempts to drive the Germans from their trenches south-east of La Boisselle finally came to fruition. The first attempt was made by bombers of 7th East Lancs, who were repulsed, but a subsequent direct infantry assault over the open was completely successful.

Probably taken at the same time as that showing the bombers in Avoca Valley, this picture shows a number of machine gun teams moving forward in the vicinity of La Boisselle.

The Position on the morning of 7th July, south of Contalmaison

As on the 4th, the weather during 7th July 1916 was miserable. The Official History[13] reports that,

> 'The trenches became knee-deep, in some cases waist-deep, in clinging slime, and, under shellfire, collapsed beyond recognition. Movement was often an agony: men fainted from sheer exhaustion whilst struggling through deep mud; in some localities a team of fourteen horses was required to bring up a single ammunition wagon. Under such handicaps, the advance of reinforcements and the circulation of orders suffered grave delay; and on many occasions artillery barrages were called for in vain, so frequently did hostile bombardments cut telephone lines in the forward areas where there had been no time to bury them.'

These were the sort of conditions which popular memory has associated with Passchendaele in the autumn and early winter of late 1917, yet this was the Somme in mid-summer 1916! In this context I have concentrated upon the events which the 12th Manchesters passed through at this time. This battalion was to play a significant part in the attacks upon Quadrangle Support and Pearl Alley, both trenches lying in the valley between Contalmaison and Mametz Wood. XV Corps was of the opinion that if these two trenches were captured the subsequent fight for Mametz Wood and Contalmaison would be made much easier. The memorial, erected to the memory of the 12th Manchester's men, to be found at the back of Contalmaison's communal cemetery, is a fine vantage point from which to visualise these events.

The 12th Manchesters were part of the 17th (Northern) Division. Their Brigade, the 52nd, had moved up to take over positions north of Fricourt in the late evening of 3rd July. That night the sunken lane leaving Fricourt towards Contalmaison was terribly congested with troops and it was fortunate that the German artillery was not aware of the five battalions crowded onto this short stretch of track. This moment was one of the great missed opportunities of the Somme battle in that British patrols had found both Mametz Wood and Quadrangle Trench empty that afternoon. This extraordinary situation did not last for long and subsequent attacks by the 7th Division on Mametz Wood and the 17th Division on Quadrangle Trench, which lay between the southern tip of Mametz Wood and Contalmaison, were necessary. As we have already seen these attacks did improve the British position although Mametz Wood still held. During these attacks, on the night of 4/5th July, two battalions of 52 Brigade, the 10th Lancashire Fusiliers and the 9th Northumberland Fusiliers, took and consolidated Quadrangle Trench. On the night of 5th July the 7th Division, on the right around

Mametz Wood, was replaced by the 38th (Welsh) Division whose link with subsequent events in Mametz Wood is well known.

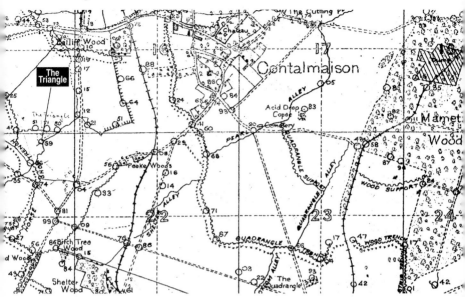

Map 12. Part of an original trench map showing the scene of the attacks made by the 12th Manchesters on the morning of 7th July 1916. Quadrangle Support is the trench which initially runs parallel to the track between Contalmaison communal cemetery and the wood shown as The Quadrangle, which lies between Bottom Wood and Mametz Wood.

The plan of attack on Quadrangle Support, and Pearl Alley beyond, which the 17th Division was then ordered to follow by Lieutenant-General Horne was, at best, seriously flawed. Major-General Pilcher of 17th Division complained that even if these trenches were taken they could never be held whilst under the cross fire of machine guns in Mametz Wood and the vicinity of Contalmaison. Nevertheless, at 2.00 am in the complete darkness of the early morning of 7th July, following a 35 minute bombardment fired rather inaccurately on map co-ordinates, the 10th Lancashire Fusiliers and 9th Northumberland Fusiliers attempted to capture Quadrangle Support. Those bleak early morning hours were marked by torrential rain-showers and the attack was destined to fail, although some members of the Lancashire Fusiliers did manage to penetrate as far as Pearl Alley and the wreckage of Contalmaison. However, they were driven out by a determined counter attack by the Lehr Regiment and bombers of the 9th Grenadiers.

81

The view towards Mametz Wood from the site of the 12th Manchester's memorial within Contalmaison's communal cemetery.

Later, the Corps' order for a renewed attack was only received by the 17th Division at 5.25 am, but telephone links forward of Brigade HQs were utterly unreliable. Consequently it was only at about 7.00 am that the 12th Manchesters were called up from their reserve trenches, further back on the Fricourt – Contalmaison road. As a result it was more than six hours after the initial and failed assault by the two battalions of Fusiliers, at approximately 8.03 am, that the 12th Manchesters and two companies of the 9th Duke of Wellingtons advanced towards Acid Drop Copse, the site of which is clearly visible just yards to the east from the battalion's memorial, and Quadrangle Support Trench, in clear daylight under a now cloudless sky. The artillery bombardment which preceded this attack had still produced no discernible damage to Quadrangle Support Trench or its wire and to make matters worse the communication difficulties forward of Brigade headquarters had ensured that the men's assault was a few minutes late.

Having formed up behind the hedge running west from Bottom Wood the 12th Manchesters had attacked across Quadrangle Trench, still occupied by other battalions of 52 Brigade. The delays meant that the Manchester soldiers lost any protection from their own barrage which had now shifted forward, leaving the German troops who were defending Quadrangle Support able to deliver a withering rifle fire in the face of the attackers. 52 Brigade's objective was 700 metres distant and as soon as the men showed themselves on the higher ground overlooking Quadrangle Support they were devastated by severe machine gun fire, mostly coming from Mametz Wood on the right, suffering 16 officer casualties and 539 amongst the men. The few survivors were later brought back under the supervision of their commanding officer, Lieutenant Colonel E.G.Harrison. A few posts remained out and they were engaged all day long in skirmishes with enemy bombing parties. Only two officers remained unwounded. Major-General Pilcher's concerns had come, terribly and fully, to realisation. It was a catastrophic end to one of the first service battalions raised in Manchester on the outbreak of war. Hereafter the drafts which replaced the casualties were drawn from many other localities and the Manchester character of the battalion was diluted. One of those wounded that morning was Major Browell who would unveil the original memorial eleven years later.

The Official History of the Somme Battle apportions blame for the missed opportunities of 3rd July to the leadership of XV Corps, Lieutenant General Horne. It states clearly that:

'It would appear that if the XV Corps had encouraged more vigorous action on the afternoon of the 3rd, a hold on Mametz Wood could have been secured, and Wood Trench and Quadrangle Trench occupied. The last-named objective was taken on the morning of the 5th, but the others were to cost many lives and much precious time.'[14]

Many of those lives lost belonged to the men serving with the 12th Manchesters and the memorial at Contalmaison is a fitting tribute to their unswerving devotion to duty.

Whilst not delving too far into the fighting around Mametz Wood on the 7th July it is worth noting that the attacks undertaken there, by XV Corps, came to nought. However, this day did witness some extraordinary events in the attempts to take Contalmaison by the 19th and 23rd Divisions as well as Ovillers by the 12th Division[15].

East of La Boisselle the 19th Division's men advanced a considerable distance during an attack undertaken at 8.15 am on the morning of 7th July. The objective of this attack was a trench a little way west of Bailiff Wood, which faced Contalmaison across 400 yards of shallow valley. It is worth noting here that before the war Bailiff Wood had been planted with saplings which were, even by 1916, little more than a few feet high. The wood therefore did not provide any sort of shelter from observation. Before 10.00 am three battalions had captured the whole of these positions, in the process taking prisoner over 400 German soldiers from no less than six regiments and five divisions!

To the right of the 19th Division the men of the 23rd Division made the first systematic assault on Bailiff Wood and Contalmaison village. On the left of 23rd Division's attack 68 Brigade was due to capture Bailiff Wood, whilst on their right 24 Brigade was to capture the village of Contalmaison. 68 Brigade's attack was undertaken by the 11th Northumberland Fusiliers at 9.15 am, supported by the 12th Durham Light Infantry. The Divisional narrative of these events describes the situation here as, 'difficult as the rain had flooded the country and the men were waist deep in mud'. Whilst these two battalions achieved considerable success, unfortunately without being able to complete the capture of Bailiff Wood, the most remarkable advance was achieved by the 1st Worcesters. This battalion was due to attack Contalmaison from Pearl Alley at 8.00 am, with the aid of the 2nd East Lancs on their left. These attacks were to be contingent upon a successful night attack by 52 Brigade on the northern end of Pearl Alley and Quadrangle Support Trench.

As already seen that night attack failed and it was not until between 9 and 10.00 am that the Pearl Alley trench was controlled by the fire of 52 Brigade. Prior to that moment much of the British artillery was firing on positions held by the Worcesters, causing many casualties in B and C Companies and causing a temporary retirement of C Company from the northern end of Shelter Alley. Even the sending up of an array of Verey lights failed to attract the attention of the artillery's observers and many of the men were upset at this example of 'friendly fire' casualties. However reports were then received from artillery observers by the 1st Worcester's HQ that 'Bailiff Wood and the Northern portion of Contalmaison were held by our troops'. These reports subsequently proved to be false and without foundation, but 'orders were received by us to at once proceed with the attack on Contalmaison from the south'. The Worcesters therefore deployed at 10.00 am from the southern end of Pearl Alley with the East Lancs moving slowly on their left from the area of Peake Woods. Unfortunately the East Lancs were soon bogged down by the combined effects of the mud in the valley and the machine gun fire coming from both Contalmaison and the as yet uncaptured Bailiff Wood. However, the Worcesters pressed on alone, breasting the slope and forcing their way into Contalmaison's wreckage. B Company was the first to arrive, taking 75 prisoners as they bombed their way towards the church. Later when C Company had got into position two German counter attacks were repulsed as close quarter and hand to hand fighting continued. For much of this period the German artillery shelled the village with an utter disregard for whoever was in control. By 1.00 pm D Company came up in support and for a while these three companies of the Worcesters fought on in Contalmaison, unaided. Disastrously, within minutes of D Company's arrival, the weather broke again. The Worcester's diary records that,

'... the rain came down in torrents, flooding communication trenches, and rendering the ground slippery and nigh impassable to any speedy reinforcement. The results of these circumstances were that the Germans from 2.00 pm onwards, assisted by heavy shellfire, beat us back steadily out of Contalmaison, the battalion being then quite unsupported had heavy losses and by 5.00 pm the whole were back in Shelter Alley.'[16]

That afternoon the 23rd Division's HQ staff accepted that owing to the state of the ground it was impossible to carry out another attack to recapture Contalmaison. Nor was a night time attack feasible. At the close of the day, here at Contalmaison, the 68th Brigade established a line, facing the village on the west, with the 24th Brigade almost in touch on their right, south of the village.

The Position on the morning of 7th July, west of Ovillers

North of Ovillers X Corps, now part of Gough's Reserve Army, was under attack from the early hours of the morning. In the lodgement just north of Thiepval and at Leipzig Redoubt the British troops were being hard pressed by German attempts to recover these two positions. But here at Ovillers the southern arm of General Gough's Reserve Army was due to advance, using 74 Brigade (attached to the12th from the 25th Division) and 36 Brigade (12th Division) to attack the village. New assembly trenches had been dug for 36 Brigade's attack, 300 yards from the German front line positions. The attack of 74 Brigade, from south of Ovillers across the head of Mash Valley, was led at 8.00 am by the 9th Loyal North Lancs and the 13th Cheshires. These two battalions reached the first German trench but no further progress could be developed in view of the horrendous officer and NCO casualties. In the face of continuing unremitting machine gun fire the surviving men occupied the German trenches on the south-west side of Ovillers. Meanwhile 36 Brigade's men were being pounded by a great weight of artillery fire falling on the new assembly trenches. In these confines the men of the 7th Royal Sussex and the 8th and 9th Royal Fusiliers had already taken almost 300 casualties. However, these men's blood was up and in a furious assault at 8.30 am the three battalions carried the first three lines of German trenches, capturing a great number of prisoners. No quarter was given in this terrible fight. The men of 36 Brigade lost over 1,400 killed or wounded that morning in taking the western outskirts of Ovillers. Terribly thinned in number the men could

This fine photograph shows a Lewis Gunner posing for the official photographer at Ovillers.

not hold the third line of German trenches so the second line was consolidated, leaving some outposts in front.

As at Contalmaison, the afternoon brought heavy rain making the tasks of consolidation, evacuation of the wounded and the bringing up of supplies and reinforcements a Herculean task. Nevertheless, that afternoon Haig was at Reserve Army HQ and pressed Gough to complete the capture of Ovillers as soon as possible, linking on his right with the progress made at La Boisselle by III Corps. A further attack on Ovillers was therefore organised, timed for 3.45 am on the morning of 8th July.

The Position on the morning of 8th July, at Ovillers

During the first twelve hours of the 8th July the troops of the 12th Division in the form of 36 Brigade continued their efforts in the depth of the utter quagmire which Ovillers had become. During the darkness these men had been reinforced by the 7th East Surreys and the 9th Essex, allowing an advance of 200 yards into the village to be made. From their trenches at the head of Mash Valley the 13th Cheshires, together with the 2nd Royal Irish Rifles and the 8th South Lancashires, had bombed their way forward and turned east, securing the trench which ran towards the crumpled vestiges of the village church.

Men belonging to the 13th Royal Fusiliers at rest behind the Tara-Usna lines after their capture of a trench which ran into the northern end of Ovillers during the late evening of 8th July. In the foreground are a number of French Artillerymen. The photograph was taken in the vicinity of Bapaume Post cemetery and the industrial estate now springing up on the eastern borders of Albert. When this image was captured the slopes here were described as 'thick with the infantry of four or five divisions..... In between the lumps of infantry British 18 pounders and French 75s, tucked into shallow emplacements, were cracking and banging. A 60 pounder at the side of the road stirred the dust into whorls at each discharge; horses passed by, shied and fled up the hill. There was a dressing-station by our side to which Ford ambulances came and went unceasingly and unhurriedly. Once or twice German shells fired blindly exploded on the road. In the morning sun every figure, every stunted tree, was illuminated with a clarity of outline as in a Manet picture. The round white rumps of men seated on latrines facing the town added points of light to the drab tint of the worn grass, the baked leaves and the dusty creamy track. The crowd shifted and heaved. But for the guns spitting and flashing and the half naked men, it might have been Parliament Hill on an August Bank Holiday.' [Guy Chapman. 13th Royal Fusiliers.]

Later in the day, at 8.00 pm, the 74th Brigade renewed its attacks against the southern flank of Ovillers, making considerable progress northwards through this part of the village which was found to contain relatively few unwounded German troops. Amongst the British troops here it was generally held that Ovillers and possibly Pozieres beyond could have been taken this night. Unfortunately no reserves were available to exploit the palpable weakness of the German situation. The 12th Division, which had been here since their arrival on the terrible night of the 1st/2nd July, were exhausted and in the process of being relieved by 14 Brigade of the 32nd Division[17]. One interesting comment gleaned from the 25th Division's Commanding Officer's War Diary gives an insight into the incomprehensible complexities being faced by the infantry on the ground. Even by a charitable interpretation of the diary it seems the Divisional Commander, Major General E.G.T. Bainbridge, lacks confidence in at least two of his Brigadiers, not to mention the organisational capabilities of his superior officers.

'The situation when G.O.C. 25th Division assumed command South of Ovillers was obscure. 32nd Division was not certain exactly what line it held in Ovillers; – 75th Infantry Brigade and 19th Divisions positions were clear, but 74th Infantry Brigade reported itself on a certain line whereas it was actually in advance of this line. Officers in this latter Brigade did not appear capable of reading their maps. G.O.C.s 74th and 75th Infantry Brigades also had not been up to view the situation and ground, and consequently lacked clear understanding... The Ovillers operations lacked sting on account of the absence of a definite co-ordinated policy, and deteriorated into desultory trench fighting operations – attempts being made to gain ground eastwards towards Pozieres and northwards to Ovillers at the same time. The Army, Corps, and Division were all strangers to each other, and the experience gathered from these Ovillers operations was, that Divisions cannot be shifted about from Corps to Corps if mutual understanding and confidence are to exist.'[18]

The events of 8th - 11th July at Contalmaison

By the morning of the 8th July the mud within the trenches south and west of Contalmaison was so thick and deep that men could not move in their depths. Many became stuck fast, unable to get out without assistance. Above ground conditions were little better. The Germans however were still in active control of both Contalmaison and Bailiff Wood. Attempts to make contact between 24 Brigade, south of the village, and 68 Brigade to the west were continually thwarted. The 1st

Worcesters made another brave attempt on the village in the evening but were stopped by machine gun fire and a heavy barrage. A similar attempt by the 2nd Northamptonshires to advance from Peake Woods across the western face of the village, in an attempt to join with 68 Brigade near Bailiff Wood, was also unsuccessful.

The following morning, the 9th July, the situation was changed by the successful attacks made by soldiers belonging to 69 Brigade. Men of the 10th Duke of Wellingtons (attached to 24 Brigade) established a machine gun post just south of Contalmaison which could sweep the whole area with its fire. The 12th Durham Light Infantry gradually wrested control of Bailiff Wood following their attack at 8.15 pm. Hand to hand fighting continued within Bailiff Wood well past nightfall and the advantage gained was crucial in the forthcoming assault on the village, now ordered for the following day. That attack was to be undertaken by the 8th and 9th battalions of the Yorkshire Regiment (Green Howards) together with two companies of the 11th West Yorkshires who would make a flanking attack from Bailiff Wood.

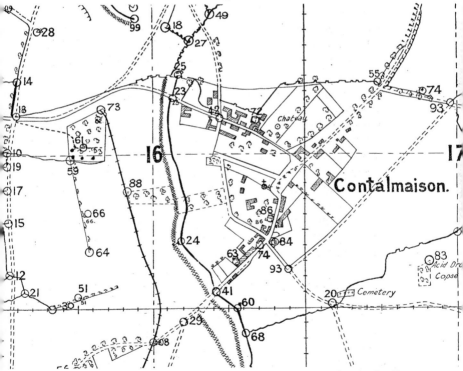

Map 13. This 1:5,000 scale map shows the area around Contalmaison in detail. Portion of 57.d.SE. Sheet 2.

The village of Contalmaison viewed from the vicinity of Peake Woods to the south-west.

On the morning of 10th July the 8th and 9th Yorkshires were assembled in Horseshoe Trench, some 1,200 yards west of Contalmaison. The village and the trench in front of it were subjected to an intense artillery bombardment between 4 and 4.30 pm. As the infantry attack developed the artillery was due to move, in five short lifts, through the village and then rest on its eastern side. Simultaneously it was planned to fire a smoke screen from the brigade's Stokes mortars in Bailiff Wood, but time and mud prevented sufficient ammunition from being carried up to fire an adequate screen. Nevertheless, at 4.30[19] the Yorkshire infantry moved forward, in four waves. The 9th Battalion were on the left with the 8th on their right. The 9th Battalion in particular had a hard task, having to cross over 1000 yards of open ground under intense shrapnel fire coming from Contalmaison Wood. When about 500 yards from Contalmaison heavy machine gun and rifle fire was also opened on both battalion's men from the front and from their left flank. The men however were immensely determined and carried the trench on the west side of the village in a bayonet charge, at which point the surviving Germans ran back into the wreckage to continue its defence from that cover. The 9th Yorks had arrived first, the 8th battalion on the right having been held up by an intact barrier of barbed wire. Once that trench was occupied by both battalions it was clear that much remained to be done. The men again moved forward, now in short rushes across a wasteland of tangled wire and shellholes, and so determined were the Yorkshiremen that many ran into their own artillery's barrage, whose lifts had to be advanced to enable the men to get to close quarters with the Germans.

As the 9th captured two machine gun posts those guns were turned on the fleeing Germans. However, the main weight of the German's machine guns had been placed in the southern perimeter of the village defences where the attack had been anticipated. A hedge in this vicinity had also been wired making it almost impenetrable and 50% of the 8th Battalion's casualties occurred between the trench and the hedge. After a brief but merciless fight the 8th Yorkshires in particular took satisfaction from taking prisoner 8 officers and 160 unwounded soldiers of the 122nd Reserve Regiment, as well as six of the machine guns which had so devastated the Yorkshiremen's ranks. Also taken prisoner were at least 100 wounded men sheltering in dug-outs. By stark contrast the 8th Yorkshires had been reduced to only 5 officers and 150 actives by this time. Amongst the dead was Captain Francis Dodgson whose small memorial is now a permanent feature of the valley in front of Contalmaison.

The flank attack, made by the 11th West Yorks from Bailiff Wood, was also successful. As many Germans fled northwards from the village, driven out by the weight of the British barrage, the 11th West Yorks took a heavy toll of those men caught in the open. The German wounded, unable to be got away, filled the cellars of the chateau at the north end of the village. By 5.30 pm the 11th West Yorkshires had joined up with the Green Howards completing the successful capture of Contalmaison village. In total almost three hundred unwounded German prisoners were taken, including a battalion commanding officer, along with nine machine guns. That evening and night consolidation of these position began, under the protection of a box barrage which was maintained around the village to minimise the impact of counter attacks. However, from 7.30 pm onwards those counter-attacks developed. The first of these came from the direction of the Cutting [X.17.a central] but the small group of Germans appeared to be dispersed by their own side's machine gun fire. At 9.00 pm one of those counter-attacks threatened to become more dangerous when a group of 40 or more Germans were seen to be lining the hedge northwards from point 93. Major Western, who was the second in command of the 8th Yorks, hastily improvised a barricade across the road at point 84 where he was reinforced by men drawn from both the 8th and 9th battalions. It was from here that 2nd Lieutenant Bell (9th Yorkshires) attacked the enemy with his party of bombers. Although this gallant act was successful in driving out the German counter attack, Donald Bell V.C., lost his life in the thick of the action. The following morning, the 11th July, the 102nd and 128th Field Companies of the Royal Engineers arrived and began the processes of road repair, the laying of cables and making arrangements to bury the dead. Bell's comrades ensured that he was buried at the foot of the sunken lane leading up to Contalmaison's communal cemetery. The letter of condolence written to his mother two days later by Bell's commanding officer made clear the way in which the battalion's officers wished to record Donald Bell's bravery. Speaking of the likely award of the Victoria Cross Colonel Holmes wrote,

'Others will have told you how well he deserved the honour, both in the act which won it, at the capture of Horseshoe Trench, and at Contalmaison, when he lost his life. His was a great example, given at a time when it was most needed, and in his honour the spot where he now lies, and which is now a redoubt, has been officially named 'Bell's Redoubt'.' [20]

By noon on the 11th the infantry of the 23rd Division were withdrawn and replaced by the Grenadier, Coldstream and Irish Guards of 1 Brigade of the 1st Division although the fine work of Lt Colonel Arthur Nimmo Walker of the R.A.M.C. was to continue here for some time. He is buried in Contalmaison Chateau Military Cemetery, having been killed on 24th September 1916.

Engineers constructing a road through Contalmaison soon after the fighting ended here in July 1916.

Stretcher bearers, interested onlookers and an Intelligence Officer surround a wounded German prisoner, captured during the fighting at Contalmaison.

69 Brigade lost 855 officers and men in the final hours of their capture of Contalmaison. The total casualties of the 23rd Division, incurred during the seven days of their fighting for Horseshoe Trench, Lincoln Redoubt, Bailiff Wood and Contalmaison village, amounted to 3,485 officers and men.

The final phase of the Battle for Ovillers, 9th July onwards

As we have already seen, there was much concern at the lack of continuity and coherency in the Reserve Army's direction of attempts to capture Ovillers. During the period 9th to the 14th July relatively little forward movement was made in this vicinity. This lack of progress was due to the various artillery units here, belonging to the 25th and 32nd Divisions as well as III Corps and X Corps, firing on targets in the rear of the German forward positions with the aim of creating disruption and damage prior to the attacks on the German second positions now planned for 14th July. Lacking concentrated artillery support the piecemeal attacks against the south of Ovillers and up the Bapaume road towards Pozieres, made by unsupported infantry units, had used up hundreds of men during this chaotic period.

Soldiers belonging to the Cheshire Regiment show the utter exhaustion induced by the severe fighting here at Ovillers. The effect of the British bombardment is apparent on the shattered parados of this captured German trench, over which the rifleman is looking.

One small incident which seems to sum up the feeling of weariness which overtook many men is revealed in the diaries maintained by the 11th Border Regiment and the 32nd Division's Commanding Officer, Major General Rycroft. The 11th Borders (the Lonsdale Battalion) had taken a terrible beating at the Leipzig Redoubt south of Thiepval on 1st July leaving them with no more than a third of their full strength and without the commanding officer who had both raised and trained them. At best the Borders' morale was severely dented and during the night of 9/10th about 100 men detailed to attack Ovillers had refrained from going forward. 97 Brigade's report on these events describes the attack as having been ordered on the line X.8.c.0.9 to X.8.a.1.3, a strongly held part of the German front line on the highest part of the Ovillers ridge, just outside the village[21]. Even under more optimistic conditions Rycroft was never one to err on the side of being generous to his men, but on the morning of 10th July, when he heard of the Borders' reluctance, his blood was really up. His diary for that day records that the weather was, for once, good. But his personal mood was bleak.

'A bright fresh morning; wind westerly. The attack to be undertaken by the 97th Brigade did not take place. The party detailed from the 11th Borders on being warned showed disinclination, many reporting sick. The officer, Lt ... reported situation to Brigade H.Q., but was told to carry out his orders. On moving to the front through very congested and muddy trenches men lost touch, so the men were dismissed. An unsatisfactory incident.[22]'

That night Rycroft received the outcome of enquiries into the neglect of the Borders to attack. His diary records that,

'It is evident that the Medical Officer is primarily to blame, showing too much sympathy to the men of the battalion. I reverted him to duty with Field Ambulance.'

The Borders diary confirms the summary justice, the 'sympathy' ridden incumbent being replaced, on the 12th July, by 'Lt Webster RAMC.' I often wonder how well the British Army would have managed without officers such as Major General Rycroft during the Great War!

On the night of 13/14th July a whole array of battalions were used in attacks against Ovillers. The 3rd Worcesters from east of the village, the 10th Cheshires from the south east, the 8th Border Regiment from south of the village, the 1st Dorsets from the west and many battalions from 96 and 97 Brigades from north west of the village. Further attacks were made during daylight hours by the 1/7th Royal Warwicks and by the Cheshires again, who this time took their objectives but were then forced back because of the heavy losses which they had sustained.

Ovillers village finally capitulated on the 15/16th July. By this time it was almost surrounded and its final defence by the 2nd/15th Reserve Regiment has to be regarded as an extraordinary feat of resilience and bravery. At 2.00 am, on the 15th July, Ovillers was attacked by the 32nd Division from the south-west and by the 25th Division from the north-east, east and south but little progress was made, the men being indeed war weary. After nightfall the 32nd Division's troops were relieved by 144 Brigade of the 48th Division. At 1.00 am, on the 16th July, efforts to capture the village were renewed by the 1/5th Royal Warwicks, and other units belonging to 74 and 144 Brigades. Fighting took place throughout the day until, that evening, two officers and 126 unwounded other ranks finally surrendered to men of the 11th Lancashire Fusiliers and 2nd Royal Irish Rifles. The senior German company officer left stated afterwards that he had only 30 men left, and that his repeated requests for relief or reinforcement had been ignored. The cellars and dug-outs were packed with German wounded. Next morning about 300 yards of trench north of Ovillers also fell to the men of 144 Brigade. In their haste to get out the Germans, who were in danger of being enveloped from the east, were forced to leave a further 80 wounded men behind there.

Captured German trench with Ovillers in the background. Compare with the German photograph on page 29.

96

The focus of the fighting in this area now moved towards the capture of high ground along the Thiepval – Pozieres ridge where those two villages and Mouquet Farm would gain notoriety.

1. The Infantry Brigades forming the 19th Division during the fighting here at La Boisselle were as follows:

56 Brigade:
        7th King's Own Lancasters.
        7th East Lancashires.
        7th South Lancashires.
        7th Loyal North Lancashires.
57 Brigade:
        10th Worcesters.
        8th North Staffordshires.
        10th Royal Warwicks.
        8th Gloucesters.
58 Brigade:
        9th Cheshires.
        6th Wiltshires.
        9th Royal Welch Fusiliers.
        9th Welch Regiment.

2. The 8th Division's artillery stayed in situ until the night of 4/5th July, the whole division then being exchanged for the 1st Division from the First Army.

3. Lieutenant F.L.Lee, 33 Brigade RFA, quoted in Middlebrook, First Day on the Somme, pp241.

4. PRO. WO95 1850.

5. PRO. WO95 1850. This Diary notes that Lieutenant Gold was buried in Aveluy Cemetery on 6th July.

6. The Worcester Regiment in the Great War. H.Fitzm. Stacke. 1928.

7. Lieutenant Colonel Royston-Pigott (10th Worcesters) and Major C.Wedgewood (8th North Staffs) both killed and Lieutenant Colonel R.M.Heath (10th Royal Warwicks) wounded.

8. PRO. WO95 2086.

9. This would culminate in the dawn attack on the morning of 14th July which finally resulted in a break into the German Second Position.

10. The History of the 19th Division. E.Wyrall. Pub. Edward Arnold and Co.

11. With one eye on the future the 19th Division's C.O., Major General Bridges, inspected and spoke to all the Officers and N.C.O.s of the 10th Worcesters, on 8th July at 11.30 am. He thanked 'us for what we had done [and] assured us that the Division would go down in History. He bade us remember that as trained officers and N.C.O.s we must not throw away our lives and should rather direct operations than fight ourselves. Nevertheless he was extremely pleased with the Division. Divisional band played in the afternoon.' PRO. WO 95 2086.

12. It is worth noting that the frontage of Gough's Reserve Army was extended to the right on the night of 4/5th July. Control of the 12th Division thus passed from III Corps to X Corps that night. By 6th July, therefore, operations at both Ovillers and La Boisselle had come to be within Gough's command.

13. Military Operations. France and Belgium. 1916. Vol II. pp28.

14. Military Operations. France and Belgium. 1916. Vol II. pp17.

15. During the 5th July 74 Brigade from the 25th Division was attached to the 12th Division in order

to strengthen the capability of its attacks on Ovillers. On 7th July 75 Brigade from the 25th Division was also added to the 12th Division's strength.

16. PRO. WO 95 1723.

17. The 32nd Division had themselves taken a considerable number of casualties at Thiepval during the 1st and 2nd of July and were in no sense a 'fresh' division.

18. PRO. WO95 2221.

19. The 8th Yorks War Diary, PRO. WO95 2184, erroneously gives the time as 4.50 pm.

20. Subsequent trench maps show Point 84 as 'Bellis Redoubt', at X.16.d.8,3. After the war his body was removed from here and re-buried in Gordon Dump Military Cemetery, between La Boisselle and Contalmaison.

21. PRO. WO 95 2399.

22 PRO. WO 95 2368.

Casualties being brought in at La Boisselle, early July 1916.

Chapter Four

BROTHERS IN ARMS

The primary recording of what was, by any standard, a terrifying and shocking ordeal for men to experience often fell to the adjutants of battalions which had been utterly crushed in front of or within the confines of the La Boisselle area. Their weary brevity tells of a knowledge and sadness which is almost impossible for us to recreate and understand at such distances. For some soldiers and officers the aftermath was an unremitting mental anguish and torture. One such man was Lieutenant Colonel Sandys of the 2nd Middlesex, who had been sent home to recover from the wounds he received on 1st July. However Sandys never overcame the feeling that he could have done more to avert the cataclysm which had overtaken his men that day. On 6th September, just two months after the opening of the Battle of the Somme, Sandys attempted suicide in the Cavendish Hotel in London. He died a week later at St. George's Hospital and was buried at Brompton Cemetery. In a last letter to a fellow officer Sandys had written:

'I have come to London to take my life. I have never had a moment's peace since July 1st.'[1]

Nine days after his death Edwin Sandys was awarded the DSO and he was later mentioned in Haig's Despatches issued in January 1917.

Later came the historians, the compilers of more considered and impersonal regimental and divisional histories, who would record the events of mid summer 1916 with the sort of detached vision which made the memory of those events bearable to those who had passed through. Frequently these histories would be purchased by officers subscribing to a limited print run, their names often appended within the front cover in a perfect copperplate script. Sometimes, today, such volumes appear on the second hand market, their value 'enhanced' by the name of a soldier who was there, and survived. But the real and most eloquent of statements is made by those who died in such profuse and wasteful numbers here at La Boisselle. One glance at the Northumberland Fusiliers' panels on the Thiepval Memorial to the Missing speaks volumes on their behalf. Although many of the Tyneside Scottish and Irish are buried here in the vicinity of La Boisselle, the greater number are marked by no known grave. Not for them the chance of a memorable footnote in the twentieth century's history, more often just the hope that their end would be mercifully swift.

Yet from within the area and time covered by this guide a number of figures emerge as men of distinctive character and leadership quality. For want of a better term they became the personalities whose charisma and bravery illuminated the stark misery of these villages' military history. I have given here some biographical details of these soldiers, not because I regard what they did as more meaningful than the greater numbers of their unknown peers, but because their names and deeds have come to stand out within the poignant drama which is the history of La Boisselle.

Adrian Carton de Wiart, VC

Captain and Temporary Lieutenant Colonel Adrian Carton de Wiart (commanding the 8th Gloucesters) is one of the most extraordinary of these characters. His leadership at La Boisselle during the evil days and nights of 2nd and 3rd July, 1916, are the stuff of legend. The citation which records his actions leading to the award of the Victoria Cross

Taken from *Deeds that Thrill the Empire*, this sketch of Carton de Wiart in action at La Boisselle shows how the war was often visualised and glamorised within contemporary accounts of the fighting.

reads with the understatement typical of so many given during the Great War.

'For most conspicuous bravery, coolness and determination during severe operations of a prolonged nature. It was owing, in great measure, to his dauntless courage and inspiring example that a serious reverse was averted. He displayed the utmost energy and courage in forcing our attack home. After three other battalion commanders had become casualties, he controlled their commands, and ensured that the ground won was maintained at all costs. He frequently exposed himself in the organisation of positions and of supplies, passing unflinchingly through fire barrage of the most intense nature. His gallantry was inspiring to all.'

Adrian Carton de Wiart lived until well past the Second World War but considering his style of leadership that longevity in itself was almost miraculous. He possessed a love of the military way of life, seeming to cheat death with ease. He was by any measure an extraordinary man. Born in 1880, he was the son of a barrister and had been educated at Balliol College, Oxford. When the Boer War broke in 1899 he gave up those studies and enlisted into the Middlesex Yeomanry as a trooper,

being twice wounded and receiving the Queen's Medal with three clasps. After that war he was commissioned into 4th Dragoon Guards, rising to the rank of Captain. During this period of his life he had married the Countess Frederica, daughter of Prince Fugger-Babenhausen and Nora, Princess Hohenlohe. On the outbreak of the Great War Carton de Wiart was in Somaliland with the Camel Force and it was during these operations that he lost an eye. Even before his entry into the war in Europe he had been Mentioned in Despatches and awarded the DSO. Having been wounded on several occasions de Wiart lost his left hand during operations at Zonnebeke below Passchendaele. In all he was wounded eight times during the Great War and also received the Order of Leopold and the Belgian War Medal.

Adrian Carton de Wiart, VC.

101

Thomas Turrall, VC

In the greatest of adversity some quite ordinary people are capable of lifting themselves far beyond anything normally within their compass. This Midlands Private was just such a man. After the war the pen and ink sketches of artist Captain Gilbert Holiday, who had served with the Royal Artillery, were commissioned by the Worcester Regiment to record for posterity the moments of bravery and sacrifice which all agreed were outstanding. One of those sketches, depicting the winning of Thomas Turrall's Victoria Cross, forms the basis of the cover of this book. His early life had been spent in Birmingham but before the war Turrall had come to work for the Corporation in Worcester. He was, like many millions of soldiers drawn into the conflict, just an 'other ranker', yet his bravery and discipline in helping a severely wounded officer is a classic example of an act well above and beyond the call of duty. No sooner had he delivered Lieutenant Jennings to the battalion aid post than Thomas Turrall was back again with his company, fighting with great gallantry until the unit was withdrawn from the fighting in La Boiselle.

Private Thomas Turrall, VC.

The citation reads:

'For most conspicuous bravery and devotion to duty. During a bombing attack by a small party against the enemy the officer in charge was badly wounded, and the party having penetrated the position to a great depth was compelled eventually to retire.

Another interpretation of Turrall's action by artist A. Pearse, to be found in a volume of **Deeds That Thrill the Empire.**

Private Turrall remained with the wounded officer for three hours, under continuous and heavy fire from machine guns and bombs, and, notwithstanding that both himself and the officer were at one time completely cut off from our troops, he held to his ground with determination, and finally carried the officer into our lines after our counter-attacks had made this possible.'

The Worcester Regimental History of the war records that Private Turrall 'was a well-known character in the battalion; and had been freed from the Guard Room specially to take part in the battle.'!

Donald Simpson Bell, VC

Before the war Bell had been schooled in Yorkshire and at Westminster School in London. He was an outstandingly athletic sportsman, capable of covering 100 yards in less than 11 seconds, as well as playing amateur football for Newcastle United and, later, playing as a professional for Bradford. In the years immediately prior to the war Donald Bell had been a teacher at Starbeck School near Harrogate. He enlisted as a private in November 1914, was commissioned in June 1915 and was only married on 5th June 1916.

Donald Simpson Bell.

Until 5th July, 1916, Donald Bell was one of many unsung and untested 2nd Lieutenants serving in the ranks of the 23rd Division. However this day saw the first serious test of their courage and training as the Division fought for control of Horseshoe Trench. It was here that Bell's bravery and initiative was instrumental in ensuring the ultimate success of the British attacks this day.

The citation, published in the London Gazette on 9th September 1916, records that, during the attack on 5th July:

'...a very heavy enfilade fire was opened on the attacking company by a hostile machine gun. Second Lieutenant Bell immediately, and on his own initiative, crept up a communication trench, and then, followed by Corporal Colwill and Private Batey, rushed across the open under very heavy fire and attacked the machine gun, shooting the firer with his revolver, and destroying gun and personnel with bombs. This very brave act saved many lives and ensured the success of the attack.'

Donald Bell was killed at Contalmaison on 10th July. Although initially buried there his body was later, after the war, removed to Gordon Dump Cemetery in the upper reaches of Sausage Valley.

Thomas Orde Lawder Wilkinson, VC

The citation covering Lieutenant Wilkinson's winning of the Victoria Cross on 5th July at La Boisselle was published in the London Gazette, 26th September 1916. It reads as follows:

'Thomas Orde Lawder Wilkinson, Temporary Lieutenant., 7th Batt. North Lancashire Regiment. During an attack, when a party of another unit was retiring without their machine gun, Lieut. Wilkinson rushed forward, and, with two of his men, got the gun into action, and held up the enemy till they were

Thomas Orde Lawder Wilkinson, VC

relieved. Later, when the advance was checked during a bombing attack, he forced his way forward and found four or five men of different units stopped by a solid block of earth, over which the enemy was throwing bombs. With great pluck and promptness he mounted a machine gun on the top of the parapet and dispersed the enemy bombers. Subsequently he made two most gallant attempts to bring in a wounded man, but at the second attempt he was shot through the heart just before reaching the man. Throughout the day he set a magnificent example of courage and self-sacrifice.'

As with many other soldiers killed here at La Boisselle, death made no exception for rank or for courage. Thomas Wilkinson has no known grave and is therefore commemorated on the Thiepval Memorial to the Missing, amongst the other missing of his regiment, on Pier 11, Face A.

Ingouville-Williams of 34th Division

He was irreverently known as 'Inky Bill' to many of the other ranks who served within the 34th Division. It was he who, hours after the attack at La Boisselle, alongside III Corps' commanding officer, Sir William Pulteney, and the Tyneside Scots' commanding officer, Brigadier Trevor Ternan, witnessed the brigade's parade at Millencourt. The Tyneside Scottish Brigade barely occupied the space which would have been used by one battalion before disaster had struck.

Ingouville-Williams was an experienced and capable officer, thoroughly committed to maintaining an aggressive posture against the enemy, wherever he and the men under his command were located. As the GOC of the 34th Division 'Inky Bill' had acquired the reputation of a fearless leader and stern disciplinarian, but this side of his character was tempered by a deep regard for the welfare of the other ranks in his charge. One incident of note in front of La Boisselle, which came to light in a letter written in September 1930 by Colonel Steward,[2] described how the General put the expertise gained as Commandant of the School of Mounted Infantry at Longmoor to good use. 'Before the attack [on 1st July], three wagons of T.M. shells had been ordered by him to Becourt Chateau, and were exposed to shell fire on the crest of the road from Albert. Two got over, but the driver of the third got whizzbanged and hid in the Communication Trench alongside. General Williams got up out of the C.T. and drove the wagon down himself.' The scene of this event lies just above Becourt Military cemetery, the communication trench mentioned being Becourt Avenue where it crosses the southern part of Tara Hill at W.30.d (central). During the bloody month of July 1916, Ingouville-Williams became the best known and most senior of the Army's Somme casualties when he was killed at 7.00 pm on 22nd July. The 34th Division's Diary records the location as being at X.30.a.3,7 on the top of the bank of Queen's Nullah which is very close to the southern tip of Mametz Wood. Moments earlier Ingouville-Williams had been walking back from a reconnaissance near to Contalmaison, round the south side of the wood to meet his car which was waiting towards Montauban. Without warning the Major-General was killed by the explosion of a chance shell and his untimely death was a severe blow to a division and an army which had already suffered more than their fair share of casualties. Ingouville-Williams' body was recovered and brought back

Major General Edward Charles Ingouville-Williams. 'Inky Bill'.

to the growing military cemetery at Warloy-Baillon where he was buried, the following day, with the fullest military honours. The horses which drew the gun carriage upon which his coffin rested were two pairs of blacks found among the number two team of C Battery of 152 Artillery Brigade.

For those interested in visiting Warloy-Baillon and Ingouville-Williams' grave the village can be found due west of Albert on the D91, past Millencourt and Henencourt. All three of these villages were in constant use as billets during the period before the summer of 1916. The low hills around Warloy-Baillon in particular were used for the training of soldiers prior to the attacks by 32nd Division at Thiepval on 1st July.

1 Middlebrook, First Day on the Somme, pp 261.
2 Davies and Maddocks, Bloody Red Tabs. Leo Cooper, 1995., and PRO CAB 45/137.

Dramatisation of the action in which Thomas Wilkinson won the VC at La Boisselle 5th July, 1916.

Chapter Five

THE CEMETERIES AND MEMORIALS

Some well known parts of the Somme battlefield are scattered with many cemeteries whose poignant vigil serves to remind every visitor of the tragedy and anguish which visited these parts during the Great War. In such places the cemeteries seem to follow close in each other's step, a constant reminder of the evil of war. The distinctive British military cemeteries draw the eyes of the casual visitor, making a number of locations memorable by virtue of the emotional immediacy which serried ranks of pale headstones brings to the place. Serre is one such location, the area surrounding and including Newfoundland Park another.

But here at La Boisselle the atmosphere is very different.

The open countryside either side of the Albert – Bapaume road looking from the Tara – Usna hills across La Boisselle north-eastwards towards Pozieres.

The lack of woodlands creates broad sweeps of horizon, punctured only by tiny stands of distant trees. There are no grand memorials searching the sky, no crosses marking the sites of cemeteries standing on forlorn windswept ground like those above Beaumont Hamel on the

Redan ridge. This area is, more than anything else, a working environment, one where the fields have grown into enormous swathes of land across which distant miniature tractors manoeuvre, endlessly, each working day. Here in summer the dust drifts in a shimmering heat, unconfined by hedgerows or woodlands. There is little shelter and the distances to cover on foot can seem, initially, daunting. But in truth this is marvellous walking and cycling country, one of the places on the Somme battlefield where you can spend the whole day out in the sun, windswept, talking, journeying across the discovery of what is, by any measure, a hallowed and remarkable tract of earth.

There are six cemeteries within the Ovillers – La Boisselle area which are described here. Four of these are very closely identified with the fighting which took place on 1st July 1916. Two of these, Ovillers with more than 3,200 graves and Gordon Dump, with more than 1,600 graves, are very extensive in size and dominate the areas which surround them.

The Memorials

La Boisselle is the home of a number of memorials. These are all self explanatory and are referred to in the text of Chapter 6 within the section entitled 'Walk Three'. They include:

1) The 19th (Butterfly) Division's Memorial.
2) The 34th Division's memorial.
3) The splendid wooden cross which now marks the lip of Lochnagar crater.
4) The memorial seat at La Boisselle.

Francis Dodgson, 8th Yorkshire Regiment

To his friends and family Captain Francis Dodgson was known as 'Toby'. His early life was based around many characteristics similar to those of a whole generation of young men who became officers within Kitchener's Army during the latter part of 1914. Toby Dodgson had been educated at Marlborough College in Wiltshire, between 1902 and 1907. Upon leaving he had been rejected by the Regular Army at Woolwich, on the grounds of defective eyesight! The alternative route was to the OTC at his college in Cambridge, Trinity, where he read Mechanical Sciences. He graduated in 1911 and for the next three years learned his business as a clerk in the family stock broking firm in the Royal Exchange. On the outbreak of war Toby Dodgson was in his mid twenties. His battalion travelled to France on 26th August 1915 by which time Toby Dodgson held the rank of Lieutenant. His last home leave was undertaken during the month of May 1916 when he made

Captain Francis Dodgson, 8th Yorkshire Regiment. Killed in Action at Contalmaison. 10th July 1916. [Fair family archive.]

plans to marry his fiancee, Marjorie Secretan, next leave.

He was killed in action in front of Contalmaison on 10th July 1916, just weeks before he was due to be married. His military service was spent with the 8th (Service) battalion of the Yorkshire Regiment, the Green Howards. Toby Dodgson was originally listed as missing. However, his body was subsequently discovered and buried on the battlefield outside Contalmaison from where it was later taken to the largest British military concentration cemetery on the Somme, Serre Road Number Two. That removal to Serre accounts for the fact that Captain Dodgson has become one of a number of soldiers whose sacrifice is recorded both on a named headstone and also on the walls of the Thiepval Memorial to the Missing.

Captain Dodgson's memorial can easily be found near to Contalmaison. Travel south-west from the village in the direction of Fricourt. A short way beyond the village, 200 metres before Peake Woods cemetery, you will see the track on your right running along the floor of the valley. This location also affords an impressive view towards the Pozieres Military cemetery with its memorial to those soldiers missing during the Second Battle of the Somme, fought in the spring of 1918. The view is particularly beautiful in the early morning when the first rays of the

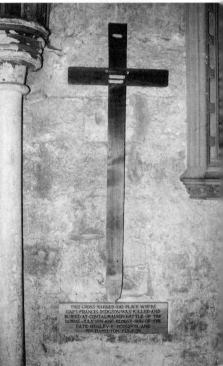

The original wooden grave-marker which is now to be found in the cloisters of Salisbury Cathedral, where it hangs with that of Francis Dodgson's brother, Guy Dodgson. [Fair family archive.]

sun's light on the colonnaded stonework reveals its depth and symmetry to great advantage. Turn onto the track and you will find Captain Dodgson's memorial stone after 350 metres.

The memorial to the 12th Battalion of the Manchester Regiment at Contalmaison Communal Cemetery.

This memorial was raised by members of the 'Old Comrades Association' of the 12th Battalion, an organisation established in 1919 and which continued in active existence well into the 1960s. The first memorial was not constructed on this site but lay on the western side of Mametz Wood. Its form was a 6 foot high oak cross, carved by an original member of the association, Ted Thompstone, and unveiled during August 1927 by Major H.F. Browell. The inscription then read,

'To the eternal memory of all those comrades who laid down their lives on 7th July 1916.'[1] That original oak cross was replaced two years later by the present Portland stone memorial after this site within Contalmaison village cemetery had been purchased by association funds. The wording on this permanent memorial had then been changed to read, 'To the eternal memory of 1039 Officers, N.C.O's. and men of the 12th Bn Manchester Regt who made the great sacrifice 1914 - 1918. Their name liveth for evermore.' Throughout the war as a whole this battalion suffered more than five thousand casualties. The present location of the memorial is therefore particularly poignant in that it overlooks the scene of the tragic attack made by the soldiers of the 12th Manchesters on that fateful 7th July, their first taste of relentless action and one in which the original members of the battalion were severely depleted. The site of the memorial provides a particularly fine vantage point from which to visualise both the events commemorated by the memorial and more generally the fighting for Mametz Wood itself.

The memorial to the officers and men of the 12th Manchesters.

110

The Cemeteries

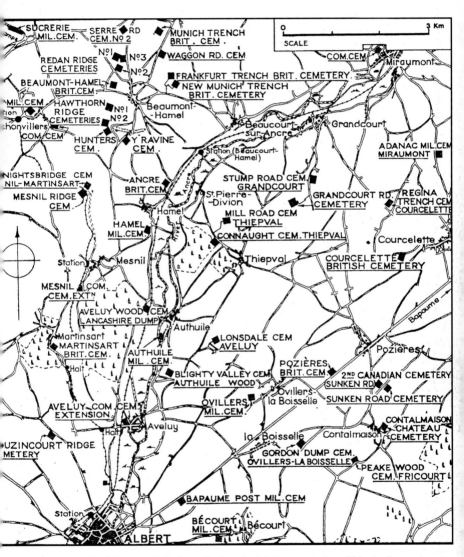

Map 14. The CWGC map which shows the location of the cemeteries within the La Boisselle area.

Albert Communal Cemetery Extension.

Albert Communal Cemetery Extension

This cemetery can be found on the right hand side of the D938 Peronne road as you leave Albert.

Apart from its road frontage the military cemetery here is almost entirely surrounded by Albert's communal cemetery. The military extension was begun in August 1915 and used until November 1916 by the Field Ambulances who were concentrated into the town, most especially during the weeks after September of that year. For two months after November the cemetery was used by the 5th Casualty Clearing Station. After March 1917 the cemetery was not used, except for four burials in the March of 1918, until Plot II was added by the 18th Division during the August 1918 fighting known as the 'Second Battle of Albert'.

Apart from the military graves the cemetery contains the grave of one employee of the Imperial War Graves Commission, Bernard Wellum, who formerly served as a Private in the RAMC. Because of the confined space available the cemetery has not been enlarged by post war battlefield clearances and concentrations. Therefore only twelve of the graves belong to unknown soldiers. The register also carries the details of one Chinese Labourer, Wing Yuk Shan, whose grave is located within the French National Cemetery, a further 500 metres outside Albert along the D938. He was killed during the post war battlefield clearances on 5th December 1918.

There are many graves within this cemetery which record men who were killed during the fighting for La Boisselle and Ovillers. These include a number of soldiers from the Tyneside Scottish and Irish Brigades, principally those killed during the month of June 1916, but also a number from the 1st July attacks including Major William Edmond-Jenkins of the 25th (Tyneside Irish) Battalion of the Northumberland Fusiliers, died of wounds on 1st July 1916. There are also a number graves commemorating miners killed whilst serving with the 179th Company of the Royal Engineers, the tunnellers who dug and prepared the Lochnagar mine. The mining and counter mining activity in front of La Boisselle was responsible for the deaths of two men serving with the 16th Lancashire Fusiliers, the 2nd Salford Pals, Samuel Hamer (11614) and James Street (15216). The Salford battalions had only recently arrived in France and were completely inexperienced in the conditions of trench warfare. The two innocent privates were killed during the late afternoon of 19th December 1915, during their battalion's initial tour of trench familiarisation duty at the positions which faced the tip of the La Boisselle salient. That afternoon the Germans had exploded one of many mines in the area of Duhollow Street (X.13.d.4,2) at the Glory Hole and Privates Street and Hamer became some of the first casualties reported in Salford's local press, their war in the trenches having lasted barely a few days[3].

Apart from the many such graves of ordinary soldiers the Albert Communal Cemetery Extension also contains the graves of a number of senior officers. One of these is Brigadier General Randle Barnett-Barker, DSO., who was killed commanding 99 Brigade during the German spring offensive of 1918, the Second Battle of the Somme. One of his closest aides, Captain Edward Inkerman Bell was also killed on the same date, 24th March, and like Brigadier General Barnett-Barker is commemorated on a special memorial, their graves having been subsequently destroyed by shellfire. Another senior figure buried here is Brigadier General Henry Clifford, commanding 149 Brigade. The cemetery register describes him as having been 'killed by sniper' during an inspection of assembly trenches prior to an attack near Delville Wood on 11th September 1916. The Official History says he was killed by a shell. Like Barnett-Barker and Bell, Henry Clifford was the son of a military family. In Clifford's case he was the son of Sir Henry Hugh Clifford, V.C., K.C.M.G., C.B. who had won his Victoria Cross whilst serving as a Brevet Major with the 1st Battalion, the Rifle Brigade, during the Battle of Inkerman in the Crimean campaign. Clifford's VC has a distinctive place in history since he received it from Queen Victoria at the very first investiture in Hyde Park on 26th June, 1857.

Henry Hugh Clifford, VC.

113

Canadian wounded being taken to a Dressing Station on a light railway, September 1916. The railway is probably the Nab Valley Railway which ran up the valley of that name (also known as Blighty Valley). Since July 1st that line had gradually been extended from its previous terminus in Blighty Valley to keep up with the incremental advances being made past Ovillers – La Boisselle and Pozieres towards Courcelette.

Lieutenant Colonels Victor Buchanan, R.Mc.D. Thomson and Roland Campbell are just three of more than two hundred Canadian officers and men whose graves are to be found here. After the war the 29th, 73rd and 102nd Canadian Infantry Battalions erected wooden memorials within the cemetery to commemorate their dead in the Battles of the Somme, 1916. Most of those casualties were incurred in the Pozieres and Courcelette areas during the September and October fighting and Courcelette is the location of the most significant Canadian memorial in this area.

Bapaume Post Military Cemetery

For a great many people Bapaume Post cemetery will have been one of, if not the first, military cemeteries which they visited soon after arriving in Albert. The many graves and nearby terrain are indelibly linked in the minds of visitors with the attacks made by the Tyneside Scottish and Tyneside Irish Brigades from this area, towards La Boisselle, on 1st July 1916. Although the cemetery has the atmosphere of a battlefield burial ground the number of graves was enlarged after the war by the concentration of more than 250 further graves discovered nearby. These included more Tyneside soldiers who had been killed serving with the 34th Division at La Boisselle. However, although there are more than one hundred men from the Tyneside battalions buried here, the majority of known graves from those battalions were concentrated, after the war, into Ovillers and Gordon Dump cemeteries. It is also worth noting that although the Northumberland Fusiliers' battalions of the 34th Division are always described as 'Tyneside' this and other registers record that many men who served within these units came from more distant places such as Moseley in Birmingham, Morpeth, Blyth, Durham, Sunderland, Richmond in Yorkshire, Darlington and a number of other towns, even as far afield as Vancouver in Canada.

As you look due east from the cemetery towards Tara Hill, on the south side of the Albert – Bapaume road, and Usna Hill to the north, you are looking at the position across which the Tyneside Irish Brigade (103 Brigade) was drawn up before its attack on the morning of 1st July. Those positions were approximately 250 metres east of the cemetery, on the reverse slope of Tara Hill, for the 26th, 24th and 27th Northumberland Fusiliers with the 25th Northumberland Fusiliers a little more distant on the left side, north of the road near Usna Redoubt. The Tyneside Irish were designated as support brigade to those attacks made by the Tyneside Scottish (102 Brigade), on La Boisselle, and 101

Bapaume Post Military Cemetery.

Brigade towards *Schwaben Hohe*, across Sausage Valley and towards Contalmaison. When the lines of the Tyneside Irish breasted the Tara – Usna lines, moments after their advance began at 7.35 am, they presented an unmissable target for the German machine gunners operating from their positions to the rear of La Boisselle.

Apart from the many ordinary soldiers whose sacrifice is recalled at this interesting location, a number of graves here in Bapaume Post commemorate senior battalion officers. One of those graves belongs to Major Sir Foster Hugh Egerton Cunliffe who was killed in action on 10th July whilst serving with the 13th Rifle Brigade. Three further notable graves are of officers killed whilst leading their battalions in the fighting for La Boisselle. Lieutenant Colonel William Lyle was killed on 1st July whilst commanding and leading the 23rd Northumberland Fusiliers, a Tyneside Scottish battalion. Lieutenant Colonel Sillery was also killed in action on 1st July whilst commanding and leading the 20th Northumberland Fusiliers, another of the Tyneside Scottish Battalions. Charles Sillery was 54 years of age, one of those officers sometimes unfairly referred to as a 'dug-out', having retired from the Indian Army before the war. Major Cecil Wedgewood, DSO, of the 8th North Staffordshires was killed in action whilst commanding his battalion at La Boisselle on 3rd July 1916. Major Wedgewood was 53 years of age.

Becourt Military Cemetery

This cemetery is not often visited but in fact remains one of the most intimate in the La Boisselle area. It is easily reached from Albert itself, or from La Boisselle or Becordel – Becourt on the Peronne road. The atmosphere is created by the presence of woods which almost surround the cemetery. In summer the cemetery and surrounding woodland can be verdantly colourful, but in winter the fallen damp leaves make a morose scene. Whatever time of the year this is a peaceful and tranquil setting. There are many graves belonging to men who were killed during the trench raids and intermittent fighting preceding the Battle of the Somme and these include a substantial number belonging to men who were serving within the 34th Division's Tyneside brigades at that time. The earliest burials took place in the August of 1915 and bear witness to the casualties incurred by the 51st (Highland) Division. The cemetery continued in use until the April of 1917. A small additional plot was added in August 1918. Because this cemetery was not enlarged by later battlefield clearances and concentrations almost all of the graves are of known soldiers, only eight being unnamed.

There are a number of points of interest to be considered. It is clear

Becourt Military Cemetery.

that very few men killed on 1st July 1916 were brought back here to be buried. However, the cemetery does contain the graves of some officers who were killed on that date, including Lieutenant Colonel Arthur Addison, Lieutenant Robert Gilson and 2nd Lieutenant Atholl McLean. Arthur Addison was killed whilst commanding the attack of the 9th York and Lancaster Regiment at 'The Nab' on the extreme left of 70 Brigade's assault north of Ovillers on 1st July 1916. During that attack the casualties amongst commanding officers were 100%, Lieutenant Colonels Addison and Maddison being killed and the other two COs, Lieutenant Colonel Watson and Captain Poyser being wounded[3].

The cemetery also contains the graves of two further commanding officers, Lieutenant Colonel John Hawksley, DSO., of 110th Brigade RFA, killed in action on 8th August 1916 and Lieutenant Colonel Jasper Radcliffe, DSO., of the Devonshire Regiment, who was attached to the Essex Regiment when he was killed in action on 31st January 1916. Hawksley had been Mentioned in Despatches three times and had

Contalmaison Chateau Military Cemetery.

been a veteran of the South African and Sudan campaigns. Radcliffe was also a veteran of the South African campaign and had been twice Mentioned in Despatches from there.

Contalmaison Chateau Cemetery

The cemetery was built within the confines of Contalmaison Chateau's grounds, to the north of the village main street. The Chateau was never rebuilt to its pre-war splendour and the pathway to the flint walled cemetery passes the grass covered undulations which mark the site of the Chateau's shell torn ruins.

On 1st July the village of Contalmaison was reached, briefly, by Tyneside Irishmen belonging to the 24th and 27th Northumberland Fusiliers. Seven days later the village was taken during an attack made by the 23rd

Contalmaison Chateau, photographed during the early months of its occupation by the German forces in 1915. Although the roof and chimneys remain intact the walls are already punctured by direct hits from a number of shells.

Division. Some Northumberland Fusilier prisoners who had been captured four days earlier were then released but, unfortunately, the village was recaptured by the Germans that same afternoon. Three days later on 10th July the 8th and 9th Battalions of the Yorkshire Regiment recaptured the village of Contalmaison. It was during this day that 2nd Lieutenant Donald Simpson Bell, VC, 9th Battalion Yorkshire Regiment, lost his life[4].

The cemetery was started by fighting units on the evening of 14th July and continued in use, between September 1916 until March 1917, by Field Ambulance units based here. The register therefore records many of the men as having Died of Wounds here. There are also a small number of burials from the fighting in late summer 1918. Fundamentally this is a battlefield cemetery although a small number of graves have been added by concentration during the immediate post-war period. There are more than 280 graves of which only 45 commemorate unknown soldiers. The cemetery is surrounded by trees and the buildings which make up Contalmaison village and, as a consequence, there are no real views to be had from its confines.

The cemetery contains the grave of Private William Short, VC, C Coy, 8th Battalion of the Yorkshire Regiment (properly known as Alexandra, Princess of Wales's Own Yorkshire Regiment, but popularly

Private William Short, VC

Lieutenant Colonel Arthur Walker, RAMC.

as the Green Howards). His grave is located in Plot II, B. 16. As a serving member of the 8th Battalion William Short would have present during his unit's successful attack on this village on 10th July. William Short survived that ordeal but succumbed to wounds he received four weeks later during the night 6th/7th August. Those wounds were suffered during the fighting for Munster Alley and Torr Trench, 1,000 metres east of Pozieres, which had begun during the night of 4/5th August. That fighting had continued until the afternoon of the 6th August when Short's battalion had taken over the attack here. The citation for Private Short's Victoria Cross records his outstanding contribution during those events, describing him as:

'...foremost in the attack, bombing the enemy with great gallantry when he was severely wounded in the foot. He was urged to go back, but refused and continued to throw bombs. Later his leg was shattered by a shell, and he was unable to stand, so he lay in the trench adjusting detonators, and straightening the pins of bombs for his comrades. He died before he could be carried out of the trench. For the last eleven months he has always volunteered for dangerous enterprises, and has always set a magnificent example of bravery and devotion to duty.'

Another distinctive grave is that of Lieutenant Colonel Arthur Nimmo Walker, RAMC, killed in action 24th September 1916. Before the war Arthur Walker had been an eye surgeon at St.Paul's eye hospital in Liverpool. His headstone carries a poignant inscription.

Gordon Dump Cemetery

This is a very unusual, almost exceptional, design. In both the style of Tyne Cot and the intimate manner of Authuille, Gordon Dump was constructed in a sequence of ascending rows of graves, here climbing the north-western side of Sausage Valley. Plot one to the right of the Great Cross is the original battlefield cemetery, but the greater part of the present cemetery has been created by the concentration of bodies recovered from the nearby battlefields. The vast majority of the men commemorated here therefore fell in action during the fighting which took place during July 1916, but almost two thirds of the soldiers are unidentified since their remains were not discovered until the post war years.

The cemetery register shows the 'planned' entrance as located at the foot of the slope near to where the track used to run along Sausage Valley. Today almost all the visitors approach from the La Boisselle – Contalmaison road and enter the unprepossessing gate in the side of the cemetery. As a consequence the architect's design has been

Gordon Dump cemetery in the immediate post war period. The cemetery has already been enlarged by the concentration of many newly found bodies. In the foreground is the trench railway which had been constructed here. [Reed]

compromised. Looking up the slope, which provides the view which he envisaged, only the reverse face of each headstone is visible. Nevertheless, the cemetery has retained a considerable presence and is well worth visiting.

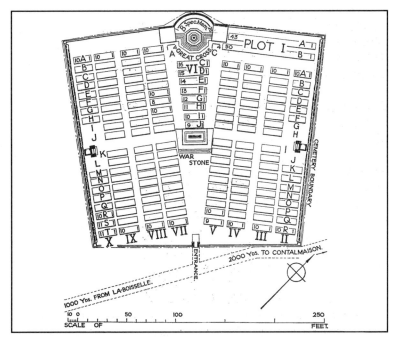

The original plan of Gordon Dump cemetery, showing the now compromised design and entrance. The gate currently used to gain entrance is adjacent to Plot II Row A.

121

Gordon Dump cemetery today.

Within this cemetery the grave of 2nd Lieutenant Donald Simpson Bell, VC, 9th Battalion Yorkshire Regiment, can be found (IV.A.8.).

Ovillers Military Cemetery

The cemetery lies just a short distance to the south-west of the village. Facing south from here you are looking across the 1st July No Man's Land of Mash Valley. The entrance to the cemetery provides an ideal and elevated vantage point and from here you can easily see where, four hundred yards south of the cemetery until those positions on the far side of La Boisselle facing *Schwaben Hohe* (Lochnagar Crater), the Tyneside Scottish Brigade attacked at 7.30 am on 1st July. The cemetery is built on the ground attacked by the men of 23 Brigade.

Extraordinarily, for a location so close to Ovillers village, this

The view across Mash Valley towards La Boisselle from Ovillers military cemetery

The frontage of Ovillers Military Cemetery.

cemetery was started before the final capture of that village, being used as a battle cemetery behind a dressing station. By March 1917 the cemetery had grown to 143 graves and was enlarged after the war by the concentration of more than 3,300 British and French graves from the Pozieres, La Boisselle, Ovillers and Contalmaison battlefields. The

The French graves within the boundaries of Ovillers military cemetery.

French graves date from 1914-15 but the majority of the British graves are from the July fighting of 1916. As is the case at Gordon Dump, a significant number of the graves commemorate unidentified soldiers, more than two thirds in the case of this cemetery. After the war the unidentified French graves were removed to the French National Cemetery outside Albert.

Three smaller British military burial grounds have been incorporated into Ovillers cemetery. These include Mash Valley cemetery which contained the graves of 76 soldiers, killed between July and September 1916, and Red Dragon cemetery which was located mid way between Ovillers and La Boisselle. Red Dragon contained the graves of 25 soldiers belonging to the 38th (Welsh) Division who had been killed in August 1916.

One notable grave is that of Captain John Lauder, 1/8th Battalion, Sutherland Highlanders, the son of Harry Lauder who was later responsible for the song 'Keep Right on 'till the End of the Road'. Harry Lauder had, before the war, gained huge fame as the author of a number of Music Hall hits. Keep Right on 'till the End of the Road is something of a requiem to Lauder's son and has caught the mood of bereaved parents of this generation in its saddened call to duty and determination. Another grave of note is that of Lieutenant Colonel Louis Meredith Howard of the 24th Northumberland Fusiliers, a Tyneside Irish battalion, who died on the 2nd July of wounds received the previous day whilst commanding his battalion's attack on La Boisselle.

Peake Woods Cemetery

This small and rather isolated battlefield cemetery lies less than a mile from Contalmaison which is clearly visible from here. Although Peake Woods fell to the British on 5th July the cemetery, directly opposite the woods, was not begun until the end of that month. You will notice that the cemetery is entitled Peake Wood on the cemetery plans and registers. However, I have used the title Peake Woods to be consistent with the terminology employed by all units and mapmakers who knew this area during the 1916 battles. The men buried here were killed on or after 20th July 1916 and burials continued until the cemetery was closed in the February of 1917. The graves are formed into four rows. One interesting fact is that there are no unknown soldiers, every man buried within Peake Woods cemetery has a named headstone, although six of those are in the form of special memorials to the named men 'believed to be buried' within the confines of the cemetery.

124

The fact that all the soldiers buried here are known has often made me reflect upon the great range of detail carried within such cemetery registers. The first entry within the register is that of an officer: 'Andrews, Maj. C. E. 11th Bn. Highland Light Inf. 25th Oct., 1916. B. 30.' Not even a first name to enlighten us. Yet by contrast the entry for an ordinary private soldier can be enormously more informative. For example: 'Richards, Pte. Henry, 14901. 'C' Coy., 1st Bn. South Wales Borderers. Killed in action 21st August., 1916. Aged 34. Son of H. and Frances Richards, of Ross, Herefordshire; husband of Lucy Richards, of 21, River Row, Blaina, Mon. Served in 4th Bn. King's Shropshire Light Inf. from January., 1899, to Jan., 1905. A. 7.' Death of course was

Peake Woods Cemetery.

no respector of rank and it has always seems to me to be one of the War Graves Commission's finest and most humane achievements to have ensured that all ranks were buried under identical headstones. However, the disparity of detail available in the registers only points to the huge complexity and impossibility of compiling details on the hundreds of thousands of men and women who lost their lives whilst serving in the Armed and Medical forces of the Empire during the Great War.

1. See Chapter 3 for a full description of the events surrounding the 12th Manchesters that day south of Contalmaison.

2. See *Salford Pals*, Stedman, Leo Cooper 1993.

3. The casualty list for 70 Brigade was the heaviest in the 8th Division on 1st July. The Official History gives the figures, by battalion, as follows:

	Officers	Men
8th K.O.Y.L.I.	21	518
8th York & Lancs	21	576
9th York & Lancs	14	409
11th Sherwood Foresters	17	420

4. See entry under Gordon Dump Cemetery and Chapter 3.

Chapter Six

A GENERAL TOUR AND SIX WALKS WITHIN THIS AREA

This section of the guide provides a series of tours and walks. The first of these is a general tour, too long to undertake except by cycle, car or coach, designed to make you familiar with the main features and sights found within the area. Primarily this guide is concerned with the area attacked by the two divisions under the command of III Corps on 1st July 1916. Because the area covered by this guide is extensive those of you with cycles might consider bringing them along. The locations around La Boisselle certainly lend themselves well to exploration on two wheels. The more detailed walks described here can all be easily conducted on foot or mountain cycle and will allow you to develop an intimate understanding of particular locations. I have organised these into a sequence which runs from north to south in so far as the actions on 1st July 1916 are concerned.

The town of Albert

Albert is closely linked with its agricultural hinterland. It is a market town and maintains a main line railway station on the line running from Paris and Amiens to Arras and Lille. Before the Great War a series of narrow gauge railway lines linked Albert to its nearby satellite villages whose produce was distributed via the main line rail network towards Paris and Lille. The town had also built a reputation as the home of machine tool manufacturing in France and was therefore a potentially valuable asset to the invading German Army. To this day that specialised engineering link is maintained by the town's motto, '*Vis Mea Ferrum*' - My strength is in Iron, and by the Aerospatiale aircraft factory at Meaulte, just south of Albert.

During the period 1914 - 1916 the station and shunting yards were within range of the German artillery and the main British railhead was therefore located at Dernancourt, south west of the town. Albert was held by French forces throughout the period from September 1914 until it passed into British control in the summer of 1915. Charles Douie described the scene within Albert having marched in driving snow from Frechencourt, past Henencourt and Millencourt, preparing himself for a first tour of duty in the La Boisselle trenches.

'We marched through Albert, over the railway bridge, past the ruined cycle factory, and so through the square under the shadow

127

of the shell-torn church, with the image of the Virgin and Child dependent at a miraculous angle from the tower, and out on to the Bapaume Road. At the light-railway crossing beyond the town we halted again under a great calvary to inquire for some promised gum-boots, which were unhappily not forthcoming. The railway line was overgrown with weeds... On our right were the remains of a house, whose shelter looked most inviting, and a battery of artillery, well concealed, in action. We proceeded slowly up a long and unpleasantly exposed stretch of broad route nationale, which extended bleak and haunted to the skyline. On one side were shelters scooped out of the banks, and some dug-outs where the tunnelling company, working in the mines of La Boisselle, kept their stores. The road was under constant shell fire, but was protected from direct observation from the German lines by a rise, on the summit of which were the riven trunks of five tall trees.'[1]

This was a march which many thousands of British infantrymen undertook and never forgot. The symbolism of the Virgin and Child became a powerful and enduring image in these men's minds as they marched eastwards to face whatever fate had placed in store for them.

The Basilica in Albert with its leaning Virgin and child – the symbolism was not lost on the British soldiers who marched past on their way up to the Front Line.

The town was captured by the Germans, during their spring offensive, on 26th March 1918. However, Albert was subsequently recaptured on the 22nd August that year, during the Second Battle of Albert. Although some buildings on the west of the town had remained relatively unscathed during the earlier periods of war the bombardment by the British artillery prior to Albert's recapture had resulted in the total devastation of the few remaining structures. After the war the town, like so many on the Somme, was adopted by a British city, in this case Birmingham.

The town of Albert also plays host to an excellent museum, the *Musee des Abris* [Rue a Godin, telephone 00 33 322 75 16 17], which details the impact of the Great War on this area. The museum entrance is found next to the Byzantine styled Basilica. The evocative reconstructions recreate battlefield scenes in the alcoves and tunnels which run under the area. Many of these tunnels were dug during 1938 in anticipation of German bombing of the aircraft factory at Meaulte. Older parts of the subterranean complex date back as far as the 16th century. The museum is open March to

The Virgin and Child which adorns the Basilica in Albert today.

November between 10 and noon and 2 until 6 pm and is well worth a visit.

On the opposite side of the main square you will find the Tourist Office [Office du Tourisme, Syndicat d'Initiative, 9 Rue Gambetta, telephone 00 33 322 75 16 42] where English is spoken. Here you can obtain details of accommodation, directions, restaurants and all the facilities for recreation and tours which are to be found in this area.

GENERAL TOUR
of the La Boisselle area

This tour is suitable for cars and coaches. If you stop at all the suggested locations the circuit may well take three hours to complete. I suggest that you make use of the relevant IGN maps. The Green series 1:100,000 Laon – Arras sheet will suffice, but more detail can be gleaned by making use of the Blue series 1:25,000 sheets, the most useful being 2408 west to cover the Albert, Becourt and La Boisselle areas with 2408 east to cover most of Ovillers together with

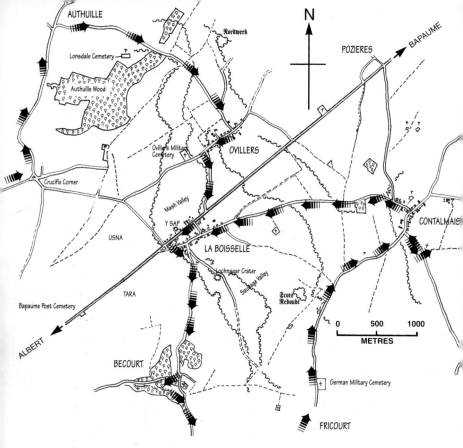

Map 15. Route map for the general tour of the Albert – La Boisselle area.

Contalmaison towards Pozieres. However, the map over leaf will help if you have been unable to obtain the IGN sheets.

A suitable starting point is the town of Albert. **Take the D50** running north-east from Albert in the **direction of Aveluy**. On entering Aveluy **turn right** onto the D20, crossing the railway bridge, then take the **left fork** in the village and continue past the River Ancre along the tree lined avenue towards the junction, known as 'Crucifix Corner' to the soldiers who were here in the years 1915 to 1918. Crucifix Corner (W.11.d.9,1) marked the boundary between the 8th and 32nd Division's rear positions. In order to find the 'front line' junction of this guide with the front lines on the southern boundary of the 'Thiepval' battlefield guide **turn left at Crucifix Corner** along the D151 in the direction of **Authuille**. Before the 1st July 1916 Authuille was garrisoned by troops belonging to the 32nd Division, and was especially familiar to the men of the Salford Pals to whom a memorial has been erected close by the village's own war memorial. **Turn right and drive uphill** past Leipzig

Redoubt (R.31.c.4,3) on your left and on towards the Lonsdales cemetery which you will see on your right. You are now approaching a wooded area on your right. This is Authuille Wood (marked as *Bois de la Haie* on IGN maps). As you drop down into the valley with the wood on your right you come to the end of the positions from which the 32nd Division's men attacked on the morning of 1st July 1916 (X.1.b.5,2). You have therefore arrived at the start of the front lines described in this guide to the La Boisselle area. From here the British front line ran south past Ovillers until it came to the German salient surrounding the village of La Boisselle.

To your left, opposite Authuille Wood, lie the upper reaches of Blighty Valley, sometimes called Nab Valley. On present day 1:25,000 IGN maps this valley is identified as the '*Vallee Marceau*'. There was a considerable distance between the British front line here, visible amongst the undergrowth within Authuille Wood just five yards to the right of the road, and the German positions 500 metres to the north east which dominated the upper reaches of Blighty Valley. The British front line skirted the corner of Authuille Wood and ran on for 300 metres in a south easterly direction before heading due south. The resultant promontory or salient in the British line was known as 'The Nab' (X.1.d.7,9) and was the position from which the 8th York and Lancasters attacked on 1st July. Tragically these men, together with the 8th KOYLI on their right, were unable to make an advance past the German fortification known as the *Nordwerk* (X.2.b). This is not surprising when you consider how exposed these men's advance towards the *Nordwerk* was to fire from the rear of Thiepval and from the upper reaches of Blighty Valley. Nevertheless, some of the 32nd Division's men managed to cross towards the Leipzig Salient during the morning of 1st July.

The view looking westwards towards Lonsdale Cemetery across the upper reaches of Blighty Valley, seen from the Nordwerk.

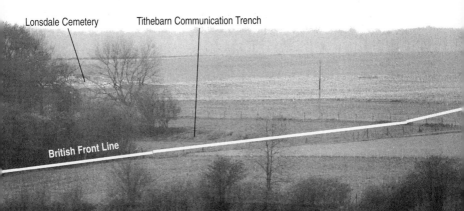

Lonsdale Cemetery   Tithebarn Communication Trench

British Front Line

Now carry on in a south easterly direction **towards Ovillers**. As you approach the higher ground rising from the east side of Blighty Valley you will see a small cross roads junction. The farm track on your left leads into those fields where the *Nordwerk* was located. The track on your right follows the exact course of the British front line for some five hundred metres. Continue along the road towards Ovillers. Approximately three hundred metres past the small cross roads you will traverse the German front line positions (prior to 1st July) which here ran parallel to the British lines. Unfortunately for the British troops who were destined to attack here the distance between those opposing lines was considerable, averaging more than four hundred metres in this area between The Nab and La Boisselle. All this area of No Man's Land was enfiladed by machine gun fire from the rear of Thiepval and many casualties amongst the 70th and 25th Brigade's men were caused by those guns. The road now continues across the Ovillers spur of higher ground from which excellent views towards Albert to the south west and Thiepval to the north can be obtained.

Continue **into Ovillers and turn right** onto the main street. There was terribly fierce fighting here throughout much of July 1916 before the village finally fell. That fighting marked the start of an incremental war of attrition which can be readily visualised in the confines of Ovillers village. Whilst La Boisselle was taken on 3rd and 4th of July by the 19th (Western) Division, Ovillers absorbed the combined efforts

The main street of Ovillers in July 1916 as seen from trench level.

of no less than four divisions which fought across its merciless wasteland for two further weeks. Three divisions, the 12th (Eastern), the 25th and the 32nd attacked before Ovillers finally fell to the 48th (South Midland) Division on 17th July.

As you can see, Ovillers is built on the southern facing slopes of the spur. Due south of the village the lower ground, between Ovillers and its twin village of La Boisselle, was known to the British soldiers as Mash Valley. Continue along the main street, ignoring the road on your left which leads towards La Boisselle. In 1916 the German front line lay some way beyond the communal cemetery which has been built outside the village. Continue along the road towards the **Ovillers British Military Cemetery** where, just a few yards short of the eastern cemetery wall, you will cross the original German front line. This large and imposing cemetery therefore lies in No Man's Land and straddles the positions attacked by the 2nd Devons on the morning of 1st July. Like most other cemeteries in this guide's area, Ovillers contains the graves of many men killed on 1st July. It is also notable in that a number of French soldiers are buried in a single plot within the confines of this cemetery. These men were Bretons from Finistere, killed in the fighting during December 1914. There is a simple memorial in the village which also throws light upon these Frenchmen's circumstances. Turn round to **retrace your steps and take the road towards La Boisselle** from the communal cemetery. On the lower ground within Mash Valley the German front line ran along this road. As you approach the rise you will see that the road is crossed by a small track (X.14.a.5,5). This point lay on the boundary between the 8th Division and the 34th Division on the morning of 1st July 1916. Go up the slope at the far side of Mash Valley and you will arrive at the main Albert – Bapaume road, the D929. Before the Battle of the Somme began the German front line ran along the opposite (south) side of the Albert – Bapaume road, in front of you, before curling back, around the western tip of La Boisselle, in a south-easterly direction.

As you join the main road **turn right** in the direction of Albert. After five hundred metres you will be able to see the site of 'Y Sap' mine crater on your right (X.13.d.5,5). Although the crater is now filled in the chalk spoil which surrounds the site is easily visible in early spring or late autumn and winter after ploughing. At the western end of the village **turn sharp left** and eastwards onto the D20 running back through the main part of La Boisselle. At the junction is the impressive memorial seat commemorating the part played in the battle for this village by the Tyneside Scottish and Tyneside Irish Brigades of the 34th Division. Before the war the village's communal cemetery was adjacent

The site of 'Y Sap' crater today. Although now land filled, the crater has begun to reveal itself again as the softer infill soil sinks. In the background is the British Military Cemetery outside Ovillers.

Below: Y Sap from the air.

to this granite memorial seat. Today the village cemetery is located on the other side of the Albert – Bapaume road next to the junction with the Aveluy road. The British front line crossed the Albert – Bapaume road at its junction with the Aveluy road, then running north westwards for roughly four hundred metres along the Aveluy road across Mash Valley. If you sit on the memorial seat and look back towards Albert you are looking towards the Tara – Usna lines. To the left of the road the higher ground was dominated by the Tara Redoubt across which the

Tyneside Irish battalions advanced at 7.35 am on 1st July only to be decimated by the machine guns firing from the La Boisselle area. On the right of the road looking back to Albert the ground was dominated by Dressler Post and the Usna Redoubt. As you drive slowly eastwards towards the houses in La Boisselle along the D20 look towards your right where the product of extensive mining are clearly visible. This location was known to the Tommies as the 'Glory Hole' since the trench lines were extraordinarily close here, being little more than forty yards apart in places!

The Glory Hole today as seen from the La Boisselle - Becourt road

Turn right in between the farm buildings onto the **Becourt road**. **Immediately take the right fork** towards Becourt. Again there are extraordinary views over the Glory Hole here to your right but this is not an area into which entry is either possible or advisable. In front of you the Becourt road rises gently towards what was known as Chapes Spur. A few yards past the Glory Hole and you are behind the British front lines which existed here prior to 1st July 1916. As you travel in the direction of Becourt the valley on your right is Avoca Valley on the slopes of which such huge numbers of the Tyneside Irishmen were killed. On your left you can see the shrubs and undergrowth marking the lip of Lochnagar Crater (X.20.a.7,3). However there is no access to

Becourt Chateau today.

that memorable place from this direction on the Becourt road. Approaching Becourt the eastern side of Chapes Spur falls away into Sausage Valley. Entering the area of Becourt you will come across Becourt Wood to your left. Extensive entrenchments can still be clearly seen from the roadside here. It was from within Becourt Wood that the 179th Tunnelling Company, R.E., began to cut and prepare the mine which devastated the German positions astride Chapes Spur at Lochnagar (*Schwaben Hohe*). Today the Chateau in the small village is used by groups involved in Albert's twinning and cultural programmes. In 1916 the chateau's cellars provided space for a Brigade HQ.

Whilst here you could visit Becourt British Military Cemetery. To do so **turn right** in the village in the direction of Albert. Five hundred metres will bring you to the cemetery which contains many of the casualties incurred by the 34th Division during the months leading up to their assault on La Boisselle. Retrace your steps and **turn right** around the small water tower in front of the chateau heading in the direction of Becordel – Becourt and Fricourt. Four hundred metres along this road a track leaves on your left. This marks the right

A group of six artillerymen pose behind a dump of 18 pounder shells. This photograph was taken in the September of 1916 near to Becourt Wood.

extremity of the 34th Division's area although you should note that their front lines were 1200 metres north east of here in Sausage Valley.

In order to continue our general tour continue past the Norfolk British Military Cemetery on your left. You are now within the area controlled by XV Corps on 1st July and briefly outside the scope of this guide. However, **turn left** onto the D938 Albert – Peronne road and travel towards Fricourt. Take the **first left** off the D938 and drive into Fricourt and take the **signs for Contalmaison**. Fricourt has an interesting history and will be the subject of a further volume in this series. On 1st July 1916 it was attacked by units from the 21st and 7th Divisions. Take careful note of the lane which lies to your left as you leave Fricourt. This lane is signed as leading towards Fricourt New Military Cemetery. Under summer conditions it is also quite possible to drive to the Lochnagar crater along this lane. However, cars are very likely to find it impassable in autumn, winter and wet conditions. Be advised that anything less than a four wheel drive vehicle is unsuitable if the weather is inclement. However, this area is the subject of a detailed walking tour.

Continue past the German Military Cemetery, located north of Fricourt, for a further five hundred metres, at which point the road begins to bear slightly to the right. On your left are two small areas of woodland. The second of these is Round Wood (X.21.d.5,5), behind which lay Scots Redoubt. According to the plan being followed by the 34th Division's men, on the morning of 1st July, Round Wood would mark a position just beyond the right flank of their advance towards their first objectives. Those soldiers on the right of the 34th Division's right column should have been men of the 101st Brigade, the 15th and

The view towards the Pozieres Memorial and Cemetery from the valley in front of Contalmaison. On the left of the valley floor is Bailiff Wood.

16th Royal Scots but they would be joined here by soldiers from both the 10th Lincolns and 11th Suffolks. Carry on past Round Wood and stay on the road to Contalmaison. Incredibly, men belonging to the 24th and 27th Northumberland Fusiliers, part of the 103rd Tyneside Irish Brigade which had debouched from Tara Hill in support of the first assaults that morning, fought their way forward to Acid Drop Copse and the southern limits of Contalmaison, the second objective of the 34th Division's attacks. These isolated parties of soldiers were never supported and the men were killed.

In between the first and second objectives along the Contalmaison road you will come across Peake Woods (X.22.a.7,7). These two isolated stands of trees are divided by an open space occupied by a farmer's silage pit. Opposite the woods lies the British Military Cemetery from which a fine view towards Contalmaison and Bailiff Wood can be had. Drive towards Contalmaison and **turn right** as you meet the village. This junction is the site of Bell's Redoubt, named after 2nd Lieutenant Donald Simpson Bell, VC, who was buried here soon after winning the Victoria Cross during the fighting for Contalmaison. You will shortly reach the village cemetery at the rear of which stands a splendid memorial to one of the early service battalions raised in Manchester on the outbreak of war. This is the 12th Battalion of the Manchester Regiment and is not to be confused with the Pals battalions which were numbered 16th – 23rd inclusive. From the Manchesters' memorial you can look east past the site of Acid Drop Copse towards the western face of Mametz Wood. Now turn round and **retrace your steps** into Contalmaison. At the main T junction in the village **turn left** onto the D20 which runs back towards La Boisselle. After one hundred and fifty metres you will see the CWGC sign for the Contalmaison Chateau cemetery. This cemetery, with its distinctive flint wall, was built in the grounds of the chateau and is notable in that it contains the grave of Private W. Short VC, of the Yorkshire Regiment. Another grave of interest is that of Lieutenant Colonel A.N. Walker of the RAMC whose headstone carries a distinctive inscription. This cemetery marks the easternmost limit of this guide.

Head **back towards La Boisselle** along the D20, ignoring the D147 road on your right towards Pozieres. Along the La Boisselle road particularly fine views towards the Pozieres Memorial and cemetery can be had on the right of the road. On your left you will pass Bailiff Wood and in another two hundred metres you will come to a small cross roads. You should take note that the track leading away on your right, in the direction of Pozieres, marks the north eastern boundary of this guide. About three hundred metres along this track a dug-out

(X.16.a.2,8) can still be seen with the indents left by the elephant iron which once supported the still visible concrete roof. At the low entrance to this dug-out a number of bricks, scavenged from the nearby desolation, were used to re-enforce its construction. Opposite the dug-out a track runs north-west in the direction of Ovillers across higher ground. The track crosses the Albert – Bapaume road and then becomes a metalled surface suitable for cars travelling into Ovillers from the D929 south-east of that village. However, this area will be the subject of a more detailed walking tour and it would be best to **return** to the Contalmaison – La Boisselle road, the D20.

Continue along the road towards the village of La Boisselle. On your left the ground starts to fall away into the upper reaches of Sausage Valley. As fighting progressed during the summer of 1916 a trench railway was constructed along the floor of Sausage Valley. That railway ran past a cemetery which was begun soon after the village of La Boisselle was captured. The cemetery is called Gordon Dump and can be reached along a path which runs down into the valley from the D20. It is worth noting that before the Great War a cart track ran along Sausage Valley, at the foot of the cemetery, from the direction of Becourt. It had been planned to reach the cemetery from that track and the architect designed an entrance on the south side with that approach in mind. Today evidence of the track has ceased to exist as farmers seek greater efficiency from their fields. As a consequence the cemetery is now entered through a rather disappointing gate to the left of the hedge surrounding the graves. Nevertheless, the best aspect is to view the cemetery from its lowest point although this means that the names on the headstones will not be visible to you.

Retrace your steps along the grassy CWGC path and **head back** into La Boisselle. Apart from the well known memorial seat which commemorates the parts played by the Tyneside Scots and Irish Brigades in the 34th Division's attacks on 1st July, the village is also the site of a number of other interesting memorials. These are dealt with in Walk Three.

At this point in your tour it would also be quite possible to visit the nearby Lochnagar crater, but my preference is to encourage you to wait until the end of the more detailed La Boisselle – Becourt walk. If you do choose to visit the crater now take note that large coaches cannot turn at the crater site and may be forced to reverse away from the site. To reach the crater **turn left** in the direction of Becourt and then take the **left fork** as you pass the houses near to the Glory Hole's multiple craters. Five hundred metres will bring you to the lip of the vast crater. School parties often visit and teachers need to be aware that the chalky sides are steep and very slippery in wet weather.

You should now drive back through La Boisselle, along the *Rue du 34ieme Division*, and **head back towards Albert** along the D929. As you cross the Tara – Usna line you will see the spreading development of Albert again. A number of factories within the *Zone Industrielle Nord* are now encroaching upon the cemetery which you will see on your left, Bapaume Post British Military Cemetery. This is the last of the cemeteries within the battlefield area which this guide covers. Again there are many men, buried here, who were killed serving with the Tyneside Scottish and Irish Brigades a mere few hundred metres from this spot on 1st July, 1916.

WALK ONE
The upper reaches of Blighty or Nab Valley – *Vallee Marceau*

This very short walk can be accomplished within one hour. Its purpose is to reveal the left flank of the 8th Division's operations on the morning of 1st July 1916. The walk can be started from the north-eastern tip of Authuille Wood (*Bois de la Haie*), at trench map reference X.1.b.5,2. The valley floor marked the boundary between the 8th Division, facing towards Pozieres and Ovillers, and the 32nd who were facing the Leipzig Salient[2].

Walk up the track, which is opposite the tip of Authuille Wood, in a north-easterly direction. The track keeps to the right, south-eastern, side of the valley following the contours a little way above the valley floor. After approximately 200 metres the positions to the right of the track have clearly been prepared for artillery. Judging from the necessary angles of inclination these guns would have been howitzers, probably firing on positions beyond Pozieres during the later part of the Somme campaign. By the latter part of the summer of 1916 the light railway in the lower part of Blighty (or Nab) Valley had been extended towards the higher ground facing Mouquet Farm. This light railway ran along the north-western side of the valley, at the head of which a small battlefield cemetery had been established (R.32.c.5,9).

Continue along the track. In places it is a little overgrown but its course can still be easily distinguished. The German front line lay at the top of the valley's re-entrant some 500 metres from the British lines. On the morning of 1st July some parties of bombers did attempt to work their way forward along this track but were beaten back by the unremitting fire from machine guns positioned at the top of the valley.

141

On the far side of the valley, in the wood marked as *Bois de la Haye* on the IGN maps, the undulations left by German trenches which formed the eastern end of Lemberg Street on the Leipzig Salient can still be seen. If you care to walk a little further up the valley you can get a very clear picture of the reverse of Thiepval as well as seeing north-eastwards towards Mouquet Farm, which was the third objective of 32nd Division's assault, and eastwards towards Pozieres which was the third objective of the 8th Division's assault.

Since the valley is fenced in you will have to retrace your steps in order to exit the area. However, that will bring you to a position from which you can embark upon the next walk, that covering The Nab and further locations south to Ovillers.

WALK TWO
The Nab, the Nordwerk, Ovillers, Ovillers Military Cemetery

This walk can be comfortably completed inside two and a half hours. The views are splendid and it takes in the bulk of the ground attacked by the 8th Division on the morning of 1st July 1916. The best of the maps to use on this route are, interestingly, any of the 1916 trench maps, 57.d.S.E.4. The area falls across the junction of four of the French IGN maps, which makes detailed map reading using those sheets very difficult. However, the map opposite will help.

We can start the journey near to The Nab at the north-eastern tip of Authuille Wood, identified as *Bois de la Haie*, on your IGN maps [X.1.b.5,2.] By the September of 1916 a trench railway line exited from the tip of the wood at this point and ran in a north eastern direction along the floor of Blighty Valley towards Mouquet Farm. However, before the Battle of the Somme, the British front line here followed the face of the wood as it abutted to the road. The communication trenches serving that front line are still prominently visible within Authuille Wood, the trench names such as Aintree Street, Mersey Street and Chorley Street serving to remind us of the presence of many Lancashire men in this sector in the period leading up to the 1st July.

Follow the Ovillers Road, in a south-easterly direction, for 250 metres until you come to a small cross roads [X.1.b.9,0.]. Following the advances of July and August, the road you have just walked was assigned as the location of a communication trench which spanned No Man's Land. From this cross roads you can visualise the width of No Man's Land clearly. The German positions lay 200 metres north-east along the track to your left whilst the British positions lay

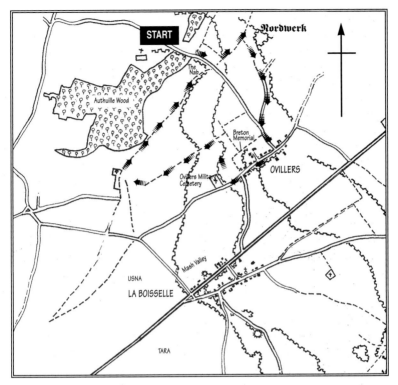

Map 16. Route map for walk two.

approximately 120 metres down the track to your right, in a south-westerly direction. Although not visible, because of the Ovillers spur, La Boisselle village lies two kilometres due south from this cross roads.

On 1st July 1916 this cross roads was the scene of the attack by men of the 8th York & Lancasters. Their assault was directed against the trenches known as the *Nordwerk*. The *Nordwerk* lay approximately 800 metres east of the cross roads on a powerful intermediate position running south, towards the rear of Ovillers, and north-west, towards the *Wundt-Werk* on the Thiepval Spur. Although the German front line and two subsequent trenches were penetrated that morning the *Nordwerk* held firm and its machine guns did untold damage to subsequent attempts to cross No Man's Land, south of the Leipzig Salient, by men of the 32nd Division.

In order to see the commanding position of the Nordwerk walk up the **track on the left at the cross roads** towards the German front line. You will cross the site of that front line after 200 metres. Continue for

The view towards Thiepval village from the high ground near to the *Nordwerk*.

a further 200 metres until you come to a **track on your right**. This track will take you to Ovillers. From your present vantage point the Nordwerk can be seen roughly 200 metres to the east, higher up the slope of the Ovillers spur. Looking north-west, across the confines of Blighty Valley, you can see the Thiepval Memorial and imagine the dominance of that position. You can now walk towards Ovillers enjoying the superb panoramic view of this part of the Somme battlefield. As you walk along the track you can visualise the German front line which lay some three hundred metres to your west. On the morning of 1st July a large part of that German front line was initially gained by small groups of men of 8th Division's 70 and 25 Brigades, only to be lost again as the day progressed. As you approach Ovillers you will rejoin the road which runs between The Nab and Ovillers village.

Walk into Ovillers, on the road running from The Nab, ignoring the small road on your right which skirts the northern side of the village. **Turn right** onto the main street. As you walk along the street the church is on your left but its pre-war location was on the right. Continue to walk through the village until you approach the road on your left which crosses Mash Valley towards La Boisselle. From this vantage-point you can look across the lowest ground within Mash Valley where the German front line ran along the road which linked La Boisselle with Ovillers. This re-entrant was the position initially attacked by the 2nd Middlesex, on 1st July, and by the 2nd West Yorkshires in support. Here No Man's Land is more than 700 metres wide, yet quite incredibly some men managed to get across in the face of intense machine gun fire to penetrate the German lines. Unfortunately that hold was tenuous and by 9.15 am those small groups were forced to withdraw and take shelter in shell holes outside the German lines. From where you are now stood, on the outskirts of Ovillers, you can walk past the communal cemetery to the west of which lay the German front line. That German front line followed a north to south course and was situated just short of the eastern perimeter of the Ovillers British Military Cemetery. The cemetery itself straddles the eastern side of No Man's Land and lies across that ground attacked across by the 2nd Devons on the morning of 1st July 1916.

You can now **join the small track** which skirts the north of Ovillers. This leaves Ovillers main street in a north-westerly direction opposite the La Boisselle road. Continue around to the right where you will come across the memorial to the Breton Frenchmen from Finistere who are buried within the British Military Cemetery outside Ovillers. **Take the track running north-west** from the Breton memorial. In 250 metres you will come to a **track on your left** which you should take. This track runs south-west, downhill along the highest ground of the Ovillers spur, in the direction of Aveluy. Unfortunately it peters out before arriving there! Nevertheless, as you walk along this track after 50 metres you will be stood on the old German front line position [X.8.a,1,5.]. The British front line lay 300 metres south-west, lower down the Ovillers spur. On the morning of 1st July the attack along this track was allotted to the 2nd battalion of the Royal Berkshire Regiment.

The Bretons' memorial just behind the German front lines outside the village of Ovillers.

Great care needs to be exercised to make further progress since the track ends suddenly. **You will have to cross a**

field in search of the lane which runs along the south-eastern side of Authuille Wood (*Bois de la Haie*). In order to get there walk **due west from where the track ends**, heading for a small area of woodland next to which runs the lane. **Turn right onto that lane**. This is where the 2nd Rifle Brigade were assembled in reserve to 25 Brigade's assault on 1st July. Continue to walk in a north-easterly direction. As you pass Authuille Wood on your left you will see the undulations of the quarry where companies of the 11th Sherwood Foresters were assembled before their disastrous attack in support of 70 Brigade's assaults on 1st July. Due east of the quarry the British front line joined the lane and continued in a north-easterly direction on top of the embankment on the right side of the lane. You are now approaching the end of this walk as you near The Nab. The Nab is located 150 metres before the cross roads, at which you can turn left and return to the point where we started at the north-eastern tip of Authuille Wood.

WALK THREE
Ovillers to La Boisselle village, its memorials and the Glory Hole

This walk begins at the start of the road running from Ovillers to La Boisselle. It is capable of being completed inside one and a half hours. Standing next to Ovillers' communal cemetery you can look south-west towards Usna Hill (*Mont d' Ancre*) and visualise the British lines running across its eastern face and past the tip of the salient at La Boisselle. Whilst the German front line ran to the west of Ovillers village, in fact almost to the eastern wall of the military cemetery, it then bent back and ran along the road within the confines of the lowest part of Mash Valley, continuing adjacent to the road until meeting with the main Albert – Bapaume road, the D 929. Just before you reach that main road the small road from Ovillers is crossed by a track which leads, on your left, to two small chalk quarries. The width of No Man's Land in Mash Valley was greater than at any other point in this sector.

On the morning of 1st July 1916 the attacks here were undertaken by five battalions. Attacking across the ground occupied by Ovillers Military Cemetery were the 2nd Devons. On their right were the 2nd Middlesex, commanded by Lieutenant Colonel Sandys, which was the right hand battalion of the 8th Division. The boundary between the 8th and 34th Divisions was the track leading to the quarry. The next battalion, the 20th Northumberland Fusiliers, made a substantial advance from their lines near to Keats Redan, across the floor of Mash Valley, crossing the German front line trench on the slope just north of

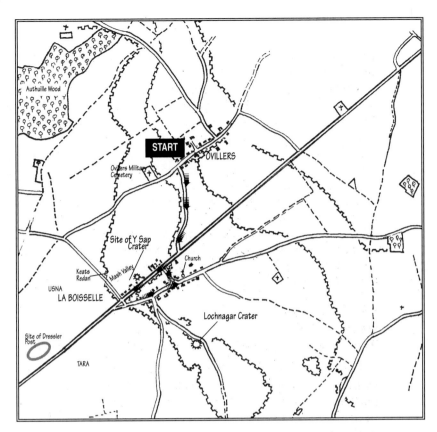

Map 17. Route map for walk three

La Boisselle and penetrating some 500 metres further to positions north-east of that village. On the right of the 20th Northumberland Fusiliers were the Northumberland Fusiliers' 23rd battalion. Their initial attack, towards the wreckage of Y Sap, was made at 7.35 am by C and B Companies, followed moments later by D and A Companies whose bombers made an attack on the north side of the village, to coincide with that being made by bombers of the 21st Northumberland Fusiliers on the south of La Boisselle. In support of these last two mentioned battalions were the 25th Northumberland Fusiliers, one of the Tyneside Irish battalions, which was assembled behind Dressler Post next to the D 929 on the reverse of Usna Hill. Their advance began at 7.40 am and few men even reached their own front line positions such was the intensity of the machine gun fire, coming directly from La Boisselle, which opposed them.

On reaching the D929 Albert to Bapaume road **turn right** along the main road. The German front line, as it existed before 1st July 1916, ran

Keats Redan

Usna Hill

German Front Line

The confines of Mash Valley from the German positions between Ovillers and La Boisselle. The road on the left leads up to the D929 and was the site of the German front line overlooking the upper confines of the valley.

along the gardens of those houses opposite to where you are stood, that is the German front line lay on the south side of the D929 at this point. Walking westwards for roughly **350 metres** will bring you to the site of the Y Sap crater. Although disguised by tons of waste and soil the crater is gradually reasserting its influence as the softer material used to infill sinks ever deeper. Y Sap was a prominent listening post and gave observational control over much of Mash Valley. Before 1st July 1916 the Germans had detected the tell tale signs of mining and the garrison

The present day church in La Boisselle, in front of which stands the 19th Division's memorial.

LA BOISSELLE
A
SES ENFANTS
ET
AUX ALLIÉS
1914 - 1918

The memorial seat, outside the village of La Boisselle, which commemorates the Tyneside Scottish and Irish Brigades of the 34th Division. The seat looks westwards towards the Tara and Usna Hills.

had been withdrawn before the 40,600 pounds of ammonal explosive were detonated at 7.28 am.

Now walk down towards the memorial seat and **turn sharp left** onto the D20 towards Contalmaison. If the sun is out this may be a moment to stop and rest for a while at the memorial seat. If you have a lunch with you what better place to eat and ponder on the panorama which is spread before you. The road running back into La Boisselle is aptly named the *Rue du 34ieme Division.* Continue in an easterly direction until you **approach the church**, outside which stands the stark memorial to the 19th Division, the Butterfly Division, hewn from blue granite. The 19th Division were part of III Corps but were not employed on 1st July. However, commanded by Major General G.T.M. Bridges, they were instrumental in the capture of La Boisselle during the four subsequent days of intense fighting here. A little further along, still on the left of the road, you will come across the village's water tower. At the time of writing, summer 1996, the tower was still standing but its concrete structure was in a perilous state of decay. To the left of the tower a grassy path leads to the splendid 34th Division memorial. Unfortunately some conifers planted in the nineteen eighties now rather block the view towards the site of the Division's attacks which should be visible as you walk towards the memorial. However, a fine panoramic view across Mash Valley towards the 8th Division's attacks on Ovillers can be seen from here.

When returning walk back into La Boisselle and **turn first right, soon after the church**. This short-cut, avoiding the need to walk all the way back to the Glory Hole and the memorial seat, will lead you back to the D929 from where you can walk directly to Ovillers.

149

WALK FOUR
La Boisselle to Becourt, thence via the spur on the eastern side of Sausage Valley past Lochnagar Crater to return to La Boisselle.

This walk makes use of the blue series IGN maps 2408 ouest (Albert) and 2408 est (Bray-sur-Somme). In order to complete the walk in comfort it would be best to set aside between two to three hours. As with all our walks in the La Boisselle area there is relatively little shade available so if your visit is in the summer months remember to take sun cream and plenty to drink.

If you arrive by car you will find plenty of opportunity to park your vehicle in La Boisselle itself. Walk along the D20 in the direction of Contalmaison but **take the road signed for Becourt** which you will see on your right as you pass through La Boisselle. This road soon forks. Take the **right fork**, ignoring the signs pointing to La Grande Mine on your left. Looking across to your right, the west, the fractured and crater pocked ground of the Glory Hole can be seen. This is where

Map 18. Route map for walk four.

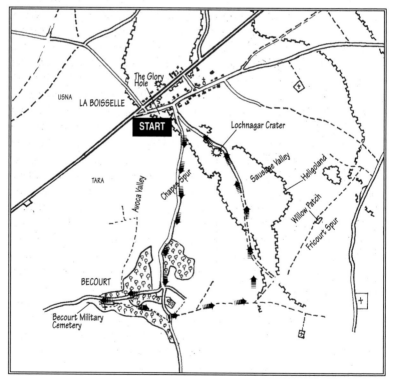

Charles Douie first saw the unreal landscape which occupied No Man's Land here in front of La Boisselle. On the morning of 1st July 1916 this sector was manned by C Company of the 18th Northumberland Fusiliers, the 34th Division's Pioneer battalion[4]. This company took no part in the assault on La Boisselle but were ordered to prevent any break-out of German troops fleeing westwards from the attacks on La Boisselle by the 23rd and 21st Northumberland Fusiliers. Running back towards the Tara – Usna lines there existed a great complex of communication trenches whose white spoil scarred the basins of Avoca and Mash valleys. Their names were invariably Scots in origin, Dunfirmline, Gowrie, Pitlochry, Dalhousie and Scourinburn streets to name a few of the many dozens. The 1916 trench maps show a farm track running up the length of Avoca Valley from the west of Becourt Wood, along the valley floor, through the Glory Hole into La Boisselle. Today only a short remnant of that track remains, near to the wood at Becourt, that portion near to La Boisselle having been obliterated.

As you walk south towards Becourt the road follows the contours keeping the higher ground of Chapes spur to your left. Further up that spur on your left you can see the shrubs which identify the lip of Lochnagar crater. Attacking just to the north of that crater, to the left as you look at it from the Becourt road, on the morning of 1st July were the 21st Northumberland Fusiliers, with the 22nd battalion in close support. These men succeeded in crossing No Man's Land and entering and holding *Kaufmann Graben*, south-east of La Boisselle. Indeed, some parties of 22nd Northumberland Fusiliers managed to advance further, towards *Alte Jager Strasse* trench east of the village, allowing parties of bombers to make their ill fated attempt to bomb their way into La Boisselle from the south. The right hand, 101, brigade of the 34th Division was then positioned from their lines facing the site of the crater and thence south eastwards towards the eastern side of Sausage Valley. Directly facing the right of the crater were the 10th Lincolns, the Grimsby 'Chums', with the 15th Royal Scots on their right. In immediate support behind these two assault battalions were the 11th Suffolks and the 16th Royal Scots. It was anticipated that these men of 101 Brigade would capture Heligoland (Sausage Redoubt) and Scots Redoubt before the reserve brigade, the Tyneside Irish, swept through en route to attack Contalmaison.

Continue south towards Becourt. The skyline to your right is Tara Hill, across which the Tyneside Irish moved forwards at 7.35 on the morning of 1st July 1916. As you pass by the perimeter of Becourt Wood, on your left, look into the trees where you can see the remnants of many entrenchments which were hidden within the confines of the wood in 1916. The shape of the wood has altered considerably from its pre-war outline. A significant piece of woodland has been cleared to make way for the farm buildings which you will see on your right as you enter Becourt village. When you arrive at the junction, with the Chateau on your left, **bear right** in the direction of Albert. This is a very evocative road in that it was marched by many of the battalions who left Albert to see action along the front between Fricourt and La Boisselle. The road is enclosed by woods, many recently replanted, which faithfully reproduce the shape of the pre-war woodland here. When use of the road was untenable the main communication trench running between Albert and Becourt, Becourt Avenue, lay twenty to thirty metres north of the present road. As you continue towards Albert you will enter the clearing at the far end of which is Becourt Military Cemetery.

By **walking outside the cemetery walls**, around its **west and south** sides, you will be able to join a small track which leads to the road between Becourt and Becordel – Becourt. As you **join that road** you should note that the Norfolk cemetery, outside our designated area, lies approximately 400 metres further down the road on the left. However, **turn left towards Becourt** and quickly **take the small track which leads off to your righ**t. This junction marks the boundary between III Corps' sphere of operations, on 1st July, and that of XV Corps to the south on 1st July. This track now leads up the slope in an easterly direction. To your north lies the confines of Sausage Valley. About 170 metres along the track you should **ignore the path which leads away to your left** in a north easterly direction. **Continue up the slope** until you arrive on the higher ground of the sloping spur which lies between Becourt and Fricourt to the east. Here, roughly 700 metres from Becourt, you will find **another fork in the track** which you are following. If you have a 1916 trench map with you this location is X.26.d.3,3 and lies on the British front line. From near this position spectacular views can be had across Fricourt and towards Mametz and Montauban along the southern part of the British assaults on 1st July 1916. **Take the left fork** which continues up the spur until you join the lane running between Fricourt and La Boisselle. This has just taken you across the No Man's Land which existed here before the Battle of the Somme and you are now stood on the German front lines of 1st July. For some 800 metres north of here that German front line, known as South Sausage Trench and then Kipper Trench, ran roughly parallel to the contours before turning westwards across the upper reaches of Sausage Valley. That re-entrant was guarded on the western flank by *Schwaben Hohe* (the site of Lochnagar crater at X.20.a.7,3) and on its

Map 19. The area around the Willow Patch. This is taken from the Official History map detailing the events of 1st July 1916.

eastern flank by Heligoland or Sausage Redoubt (in the area of X.20.d.9,9).

You now have a marvellous panorama of the La Boisselle battlefield. The view north encompasses La Boisselle, Ovillers and the highest ground of the Thiepval positions, surmounted by the massive Memorial to the Missing. During the fighting on 1st July this area to the

The view towards Lochnagar Crater and La Boisselle, and beyond to the trees marking the site of Leipzig Redoubt near to Thiepval, from the high ground north of Fricourt.

east of South Sausage Trench, past the Willow Patch and on towards the Fricourt – Contalmaison road was the scene of some limited success by men of 64 Brigade (21st Division) who advanced towards and held their first objectives facing Shelter Wood. However this is outside our designated area and we can now **walk along the lane leading towards La Boisselle past Lochnagar crater**[5]. You are now traversing No Man's Land towards the British front line which is reached in 300 metres. Continue towards the mine crater. As you enter the lowest confines of Sausage Valley you are re-entering the 34th Division's area, although now back in No Man's Land in front of 101 Brigade's positions on 1st July. 1916 trench maps show a track leading off to the right here. That track led up the valley towards Gordon Post, near to the site of Gordon Dump Cemetery which is clearly visible one kilometre to the north-east. However, no remains of the track exist today but the low lying terrain reveals the difficulties faced by the 15th and 16th Royal Scots as they attempted to cross No Man's Land, which was 600 metres wide at this point, towards the Heligoland positions. Some small parties of the 16th Royal Scots did manage to gain a foothold in the tip of Heligoland and also some of the support trenches to its rear. Unfortunately the dominant position of Scots Redoubt, some 400 metres due east of Heligoland, held firm.

The walk can now be completed by crossing the low lying floor of Sausage Valley and rising towards Lochnagar Crater astride Chapes Spur. This was the scene of the attacks made by the 10th Lincolns with the 11th Suffolks in support. It was also the ground which was traversed by those indomitable parties of men from the Tyneside Irish Brigade, belonging to the 24th and 27th Battalions of the Northumberland Fusiliers, who managed to advance almost three miles from Tara Hill, past Peake Woods, as far as Contalmaison before being repulsed on the morning of 1st July.

If you have not stood on the lip of Lochnagar crater before, its visual impact is awe inspiring. Lochnagar was saved from infilling and destruction when it was purchased by Richard Dunning in the early 1980s. Since then he, together with many others in the form of the Friends of Lochnagar Crater, has sought to maintain and dignify this remarkable place. Along with Thiepval and Newfoundland Park this crater at La Boisselle has become one of the most frequently visited sites along the 1916 Somme Battlefront. And rightly so. It is breathtaking in its size. You can almost imagine the magnitude of the crushing explosion which threw thousands of tons of earth and rock and fortifications skywards when its twin charges were detonated at 7.28 am on the morning of 1st July 1916. Memorial seats have now turned

The lip of Lochnagar Crater.

this place into a place where quiet reflection and thoughtful history lessons can be digested.

Lochnagar Crater from the air. As you can see, access is only possible from the road on the north-eastern side of the crater. Please respect the crops within the nearby farmer's fields by avoiding walking outside the confines of the crater. The vestiges of chalky spoil clearly visible on the other side of the road near to the crater are the trenches of the *Schwaben Hohe* whose commanding position the mine was designed to overthrow. The German front line then led away from the road, south-east off the right hand edge of the photograph, for five hundred metres across Sausage Valley towards the Sausage Redoubt or Heligoland positions.

WALK FIVE
The Willow Patch, Scots Redoubt and Round Wood from Fricourt

This walk will make use of the blue series IGN sheet 2408 est (Bray-sur-Somme), although many of the views and points of interest which can be seen from these vantage points are contained within the area covered by 2408 ouest. Set aside an hour and a quarter to complete this walk.

The fighting which took place in these locations on 1st July lies marginally outside our designated area since it took place within the sphere of operations of XV Corps, being attacked by men belonging to the 21st Division. However, the geographic features provide an excellent viewpoint from which to study the fighting at La Boisselle. A suitable start can be made from the lane which leaves the D147 Fricourt to Contalmaison road, signposted in the direction of Fricourt New Military Cemetery. **After 250 metres** you should take the **right fork** and follow the lane as it rises towards the higher ground. This spur of higher ground lies to the south-east of Sausage Valley. Although there was no village to fortify here the German Army had made extensive use of the topography to create a very strong defensive position. On the highest ground was Scots Redoubt, some 400 metres north-west of Round Wood. Its trench map reference was X.21.central. On the western side of the spur lay the Heligoland (Sausage Redoubt) positions, some 500 metres west of Scots Redoubt. Heligoland dominated the wide expanse of No Man's Land across Sausage Valley towards Schwaben Hohe (Lochnagar crater). West of Heligoland the men belonging to the left column of 101 Brigade, the 10th Lincolns and 11th Suffolks, were mown down in waves as they attempted to cross the wastes of No Man's Land here, five minutes after the detonation of the mine at Lochnagar.

In order to reach the Willow Patch and Scots Redoubt continue walking along the lane until you reach the point where the lane breasts the higher ground, from where La Boisselle is visible, roughly 700 metres from the starting point. Here **turn right** and continue up the spur's slope along a track which runs in the direction of the small woodland which you can see ahead. This is the Willow Patch (*Bois de Becordel* on your IGN maps). On the morning of 1st July 1916 the soldiers of the 10th KOYLI swept past here towards Round Wood on the Fricourt – Contalmaison road some 500 metres north east of the Willow Patch. The 10th KOYLI were the left unit of the 21st Division. The relative success of the attacks just north of Fricourt, by the 21st,

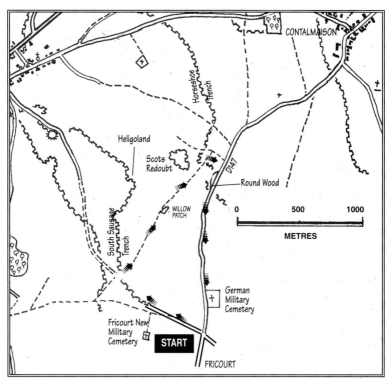

Map 20. Route map for walk five.

and east of Fricourt, by the 7th Division, made occupation of that village by the German Army untenable and they withdrew the following day.

Continue along the track up the spur for a further 600 metres past the Willow Patch. Half way between the Willow Patch and the site of Scots Redoubt lay the boundary between the 21st and 34th Division's spheres of action. Scots Redoubt was a truly commanding position, overlooking both the German occupied villages of Fricourt and La Boisselle, as well as the British held village of Becourt to the south-west. On the morning of 1st July the redoubt here was the scene of intense fighting as men of both 101 and 103 Brigades sought to wrest control from its defenders. To the north other small bands of men belonging to the 24th and 27th Northumberland Fusiliers advanced in ever dwindling numbers towards Contalmaison. Indeed, at times the redoubt was all but surrounded yet still held firm. This is a fine location to stay a while in order to contemplate the complexity of the battlefields visible from this position.

The view across Becourt chateau, in the direction of Albert, from the German positions below the Willow Patch. Albert's Basilica can be seen clearly on the horizon.

In order to complete the walk continue north-east for a little distance until the track turns sharp right to join the Contalmaison – Fricourt road. Turn right onto that road and walk back towards Fricourt along the sunken lane. The first trees you come to on your right are Round Wood, from where Scots Redoubt lies 400 metres to the north-west. As you return to Fricourt the very substantial German military cemetery can be seen to your left.

WALK SIX
Peake Woods, Contalmaison, Bailiff Wood, Gordon Dump Cemetery

This walk will also make use of the blue series IGN sheet 2408 est (Bray-sur-Somme). To complete the circuit on foot would take between two and two and a half hours and you would be wise to take sandwiches and a decent flask to refresh yourself with. The walk behind the German pre -1st July positions and across the subsequent battlefield west of Contalmaison provides an opportunity to get away from the constant presence of visitors to the area of Lochnagar crater and the Glory Hole. If you can complete the whole walk it is one of the most satisfying and pleasurable that I know in the British sector of the 1916 Somme battlefield.

A suitable starting point is the Fricourt to Contalmaison road, the D147, on the slope leading down towards **Peake Woods** cemetery. **Park adjacent to the cemetery** and you can look across the valley, marked as Vallee St. Leger on your IGN map, north eastwards towards Contalmaison village. On the morning of 1st July 1916 small parties of men from the 24th and 27th Northumberland Fusiliers managed to cross this valley before being repulsed or killed on the outskirts of the village. En route they had fought their way north of Scots Redoubt and had crossed Bloater Trench, Horseshoe Trench and the Triangle, gradually losing men and contact with those Tyneside Irish comrades amongst whom they had set off from Tara Hill at 7.30 that morning. Alone and desperate most of the tiny band of survivors from this extraordinary group were finally killed in the fields across which you are looking near Peake Woods.

Carry on along the road towards Contalmaison. On your left is the track running along the valley floor which leads to a small memorial erected to the memory of Francis Dodgson, 8th Yorks Regiment (see Chapter 5). If you have not already visited this site now is the chance to do so, looking northwards towards the Pozieres Military Cemetery and 1918 Memorial to the Missing. A short distance past the small stone

Map 21. Route map for walk six.

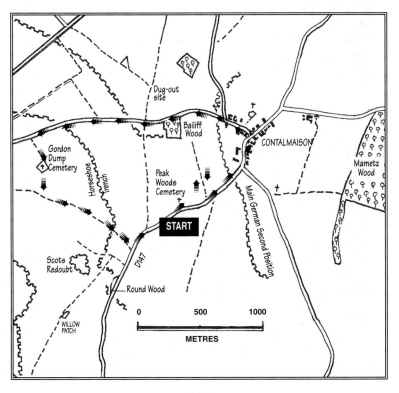

159

The stone memorial to Francis Dodgson, 8th Yorkshires, with the spire of Contalmaison Church visible on the skyline to the east. The stone has been moved a short distance from its original location on the western side of the valley. The move to the track in the foot of the valley is both a convenience for the farmers and a way of ensuring the preservation of this unique and intimate private memorial, originally established by Captain Dodgson's heartbroken mother after her visit to the area in 1919.

Captain 'Toby' Francis Dodgson's original grave. The photograph was taken in the spring of 1917, by Captain Humphrey Secretan who was the brother of Francis Dodgson's fiancee. In the background the slopes of Bailiff Wood can be made out quite clearly. The cross which marks this grave now hangs in Salisbury Cathedral cloisters. (See page 108-9) [Fair family archive.]

memorial, to the left of the track is Bailiff Wood which we will visit later during this walk. In pre war days the valley floor was crossed by a narrow gauge railway which connected Contalmaison with Bazentin, Martinpuich and Pozieres. Continue along the road towards Contalmaison. Just outside the village you will cross the main German Second Position which was the second objective of the attack on La Boisselle on the 1st July 1916. The village was the site of the headquarters of the 28th Reserve Division whose troops were defending the La Boisselle sector on 1st July. As you enter the village a lane leads off to the right in the direction of the communal cemetery, within the grounds of which lies the memorial to the 12th Battalion of the Manchester Regiment. The junction is the site of Bell's Redoubt, named after 2nd Lieutenant Donald Bell, VC. If you have not already done so, this is an appropriate moment to visit the site of the 12th Manchesters' memorial which has a commanding view of Mametz Wood past the site of Acid Drop Copse. After returning from the Manchesters' memorial walk into the village towards the church. Sixty metres past the church **turn left** onto the D20 which leads westwards in the direction of La Boisselle.

A short walk **along the La Boisselle road** will bring you to the site of the old village chateau, well known to the 28th Reserve Division's officers. The grounds of the chateau now contains the British military cemetery which was used there throughout the second half of 1916 until the March of 1917. Continue walking westwards, ignoring the road which leads off to the right in the direction of Pozieres past Contalmaison Wood. Our road now begins to slope down again into the broad confines of the valley on the far slope of which lies Bailiff Wood. Bailiff Wood was the origin of an important German switch trench running west past Wold Redoubt and thence north-west towards Ovillers. Some evidence of this trench still remains within the wood. In the latter fighting this trench was renamed Fourth Street by the British soldiers who knew this area. Two hundred metres beyond Bailiff Wood lies the *Chemin de Bray*, originally the most direct route for horse drawn traffic between Fricourt and Pozieres before the war. Here you can make a small optional detour.

If you wish **a right turn at the cross roads** will enable you to walk northwards along the Chemin de Bray until a track on the left leads up a steep slope in the direction of Ovillers to the north-west. It is worth noting that here you will be within yards of one of the few remaining British dugouts which once pock-marked this area during the fighting for control of Pozieres. A walk to the higher ground reached by the left track will provide you with a superb panorama of the Ovillers and La

Bailiff Wood seen from the outskirts of Contalmaison looking towards La Boisselle.

Platoons of men as well as RAMC stretcher bearers make use of the shelter found in the sunken section of the road between La Boisselle and Contalmaison, July 1916.

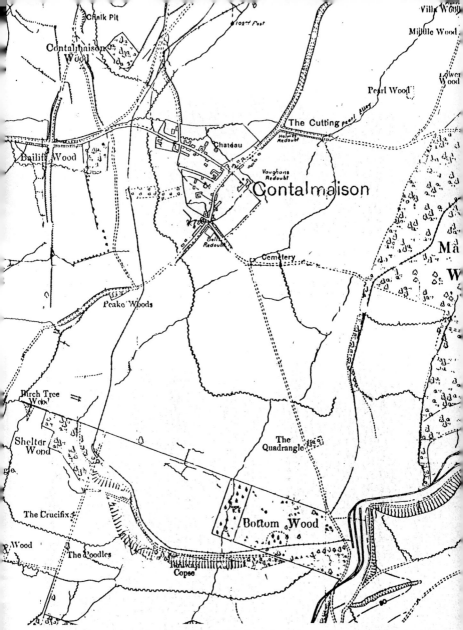

Map 22. The area bounded by Fricourt, Bailiff, Contalmaison and Mametz Woods, from a trench map corrected to 1/9/1916

Boisselle positions defended by the Germans during the battles for supremacy here in the mid-summer of 1916. On the right of this track, within a small clump of trees, is what looks like the remains of a large mine crater. Return to the cross roads west of Bailiff Wood. If you

The view towards Contalmaison from the higher ground in front of Horseshoe trench.

choose to do so, much time can be saved if you **cross straight over**, heading south, whence the *Chemin de Bray* will return you to the D147 not far from where you started the walk at Peake Woods Cemetery.

However, those of you who are still feeling fit and determined can now continue westwards along the D20 towards La Boisselle. This exposed and open road is no fun in winter with the wind and cold rain in your face. However, in summer it can be glorious as you pass by the upper reaches of Sausage Valley, on your left. You will eventually come to the CWGC sign pointing left towards Gordon Dump Cemetery. Stroll down the path into the cemetery from where an excellent German perspective view can be had of 101 Brigade's attacks, on the morning of 1st July, in the vicinity of Lochnagar crater. Carefully cross to the embankment below the cemetery and **walk westwards towards Lochnagar**, down the valley, until you strike the track which runs between La Boisselle and the D147 Fricourt to Contalmaison road. **Turn left** onto that track and follow it past the site of Horseshoe Trench back to the D147 where you can **turn left** towards Peake Woods and the great pleasure of taking your walking boots off!

1. Charles Douie, *The Weary Road*.

2. See *Thiepval*, in this same series of battlefield guides.

3. The remainder of the battalion was maintained in assembly trenches next to Becourt Chateau.

4. Although passable by car in summer I would not recommend trying it in winter or wet weather unless you have a four wheel drive vehicle with good ground clearance.

164

Index